Hessle Road Scallywags 3

The RETURN TO THE STREET OF MISFITS AND "The Scallywags" RIDE AGAIN.

FROM THE BEST SELLING AUTHOR of Hessle Road Scallywags series.

By

Ian Newton and Terry Cox

Scallywag Books

Copyright © 2016 Ian Newton and Terry Cox

First published in Great Britain in 2016 by Scallywag Books
Email: scallywagbooks@gmail.com
Telephone: 07763 840732

Ian Newton and Terry Cox have asserted their rights to be identified as the authors
of this work under the Copyright, Designs and Patents Act
1988.

A CIP catalogue record for this book is
available from the British Library

ISBN 978-0-9935547-0-4

Design, Editing and Production by Nicola Barnes, Tampa Bay, Florida, United States.
Scallywag Books of London, United Kingdom.

Printed by: Scallywag Books, (complete book packagers) of Hull and London
Cover by: Hessle Roader Kevin Ward.
For cartoons email: tina@tkward.karoo.co.uk
Printed in the People's Republic of China.

Dedication

This book is dedicated to those who grew up with us, and whom we played with, survived with, made mischief with and sometimes fought with. The great families of the Hessle Road of the 1950s to 1970s, that made the old road the legend that it was. They were truly the salt of the earth and it was a privilege and honour to grow up with them. They were the very best and the like of which the United Kingdom will never see again. And it will be to the country's greatest loss.

Wake up Britain before it's too late and think of nothing else but your children and grand children's future, nothing else matters. Our time is nearly done, but theirs is just starting, let us not leave them "The Devils's Inheritance"

Some of the great families of Hessle Road:

The Coxes, The Manstons', The Whitakers, The Butlers', The Heinzes', The Campbell's, The Sprigs', The Callises', The Daly's'. The Salehs', The Newman's, The Palmers', The Carr's', The Greens', The Stanley's, The McCoy's, The Ali's, The Adams, The Frames, The Smiths, The Hassan's, The Harts', The Bullocks', The Lyons', The Griffins', The Turners' The Greens' The Jacklin's, The Trains' The Wards, The Brumbys' The Haywoods' The Wittys' The Shaws' The Buntins, The Manouries' The Barwicks' The Mills' The Barwicks' The Moores' The Jacksons' The Hoyles' The Travis's', The Plattens', The Brewers, The Peeks' The Gwillams, The Williams' The Thompsons', The Thurstons', The Atkinsons, The Adams' The Beadles' , The Jackson's,The Beaumonts' The Marsdens, The Miltons' The Langleys' The Frazors' The Lutkins, The Scotts', The Carmichaels' The Moys' The Swains' The Powdrills' The Welburns', The Kings' The Gregg's, The Jarvis's, The Giblins, The Dawsons, The Ledgers, The Moores, The Caywoods, The Nicholsons, The Sorrensons, The Messinghams' The Hutchinsons, The Johnsons, The Thorntons, The Swains, the Beeches, The Spurgions, The Milners, The Andrews, The Dicksons, The Danvilles, The Minns, The Dukes, The Petersons, The Taskers, The Wheaters, The Kellys, The Dagitts, Hoyles, The Thorntons, The Applebys, The Joplins, The Smiths. The Bristows, The Banisters, The Dixon's, The Milners, The Pearces, The Griffin's, (To Jim and Sylvia- the very best of people) The Edwards, The Jacklins, The Shaws, The Franks, The Jacksons, The Beadles, The Hutchinsons, The Mills, The Smiths, The Lyons, The Johnsons, The Rimmers

The irrepressible characters of Hessle Road:

Pudding Head, Necky, Thick Sid, Taffy Touchwood, Sweaty Betty,
Clumpa, Duckey Drake, Whispering Jack "The Flash, Workshy Cyril
Nymphy Nora, Radish, Old Jimmy, Foxy, the "Scary" Hergsons' Old Man
Percy the rag man, Uncle Harold, Stuttering Joe.
Not forgetting, the lovely, luscious, pouting, forever gagging for it, the
temping oozing school girl and temptress, and always accomodating
when she was babysitting, POLO- Oh what nights of unbridled kinky
school kid passionate adventures with POLO.

Other books by Ian Newton:
Dustbingate
Pizza Wars
The Night Shift
Silent Backlash – now unavailable.
Hessle Road Scallywags
Hessle Road Scallywags 2 – A Brief Encounter in Hull

Other publications:
Mohsen's Rush.
The Highest Emissary
Dustbingate – The Film Script

All the above are also available on Amazon Kindle.
Out soon in paperback: 2017
by Ian Newton and Terry Cox
Hessle Road Scallywags 4 - The Search for Christmas.

Introduction

It seems many of us out there look back to the times of our childhood or teenage years as we get older, and look back more and more the older we get. Especially now as as we see our country being changed at breakneck speed and we worry about the future of our children and grandchildren in what seems a world of irrational and corrupt politicians who seem hell bent on selling us all out for their brown envelopes and gravy train.

Many will have happy memories and many of us will have sad memories, but childhood and teenage years do seem to be special to all present and past generations that get to our age, the age of nostalgia. It is the age when time speeds up and weeks and years just fly by and you begin to notice, or perceive that after a certain age, each year that passes goes faster than the previous years and life becomes a little scarier and your memories of times long gone seem ever more precious. And even if you have bad memories, there will always be those special moments of fun and mischief, and even that moment of full-on passionate teenage love that will make the sadder memories less prominent in the mind's eye of your gone time.

After the amazing success of the previous two Hessle Road Scallywag books, I had to admit to myself that I was bowled over and a little bemused by the success of the books and the continued success of the books, and I wondered why. And for someone who likes to think of himself as now well educated and experienced in the ways of the world, and a bit of a clever cookie, I found the answer eluded me. And, as ever, it was left to my wife Jennifer to enlighten me with the obvious answer. Like most men I suppose, I always like to think I am cleverer than my wife, and time and time again, my wife disproves my theory. I have come to think as I have gotten older that perhaps women have some sort of second sight because many a time both in my personal and business life, my wife has seen right through so many people, and later took great satisfaction in saying, "I told you so."

So whilst I would not admit it, I do tend to listen a lot more to my wife's opinions as far more often than not she is right and she was certainly right about the Hessle Road Scallywag books.

Prior to publishing the first book in the Hessle Road Scallywags series, my wife had always told me that Hessle Road Scallywags would probably be one of the most successful books I would ever write, and I wondered why she had so much faith in it, as I expected no more that a couple of hundred to be sold to Hull locals who would obviously have an interest. To my massive surprise my expectations were blown away when I got a call at 6am one morning from my publisher excitedly informing me, that he had just been informed by the book ratings agency that Hessle Road Scallywags had entered the best seller's listings with its first three weeks of sales.

Being the person I am, I looked for reason for the book's success and as usual I looked for the more complicated reasons whilst the simple answer was just staring me in the face. "People of our age," said my wife, "are hungry for their own humour and their own memories from our time."

Of course she was right again, because the humour of my generation, the post second world war children is all but banned now thanks to the march of the new PC Gestapo that patrols and pervades all aspects of life, like Orwell's "Thought Police" in his novel 1984. My wife went on, "Our generation arc so hungry for laughter, so hungry for real memories that mean something to them." And I knew she was right because I also miss more than anything the humour from my childhood and teenage times that is now exiled by the reality deniers and distorters of "Political Correctness." I fucking hate the bastards with every bone of my body. I think you get my drift but let's move on to some fun.

And now for a few words from my co-writer and conspirator, and old Hessle Road mate and partner in crime on this new book, and one of the original Hessle Road Scallywags, Terry Cox. Like me Terry has become a bit of a grumpy old bastard as he has reluctantly been frog marched into his older years, and as he moans about his piles, erectile dysfunction, age aching limbs and bad back. Yes, Tez is a right old moaning bastard, but Terry is at least good for one thing, if not much else, and that he is one of the funniest men I know and tells a yarn like no one else. And since renewing our friendship after more than forty years of losing touch, (I think he's been in prison) we have taken to having a regular pint or two in the Avenue Pub down Chanterlands Avenue in Hull, and having a good moan about the world. And after much drink fuelled discussion, and some slurring, ranting and swearing, we put the whole country to rights in great economic, social and political detail and write our own manifesto on the back of a fag packet as people of our age have a tendency to do.

Anyway, before Terry feigns a heart attack coming on because it's his round, a few words of grumpy wisdom from my old sea dog mate, Terry Cox. So let's hear a hearty round of Hessle Road applause for Mr Terry "Rupert" "Bartholomew" "Tarquin" Cox (The third) formerly of Rise Walk, Marmaduke street, Hessle Road after eviction for rent arrears, keeping rabbits under the sink and a horse in the back room.

Ladies and Gentlemen, I give you Mr Terry Cox, ex fisher kid and big boater after graduating as one of the most successful "Look outs" on the Titanic and, is renowned in hallowed nautical circles for that legendary and immortal cry of, "Icebergs!!! What fucking Iceberg, silly bastard!!!" Not forgetting of course that Terry was also at the forefront of the cross-dressing revolution especially when it came to getting in the lifeboats.

Terry Cox here readers, thank fuck Ian has retreated to the bar to chat up the new bar maid "Drop 'em Dora." The only women who carries a handbag big enough to take a mattress.

Thanks for the big build up Ian and the blasting introduction (and it's your round prat face) and since you graciously let out the secrets of my middle names, I can only return the gesture with equal comradeship (you bastard).

Before I start my old codgers moan, I would like to ask my "good" mate, what's all this name changing business about, Mr Ian Achmed to Ian Newton? Now come on Ian, never mind all this name changing Ian "Newton" shit, we all know who you are and you won't throw the Police off as easy as that or the debt collectors. We all know that you have earned a bob or two since we both climbed out of that impoverished shit hole, but apparently not the taxman, not yet anyway. "Now get the fuckin' beer in!"

But I would just like to say, and don't think I'm moaning, because I am sat here with an empty glass – AGAIN!, and I see you are slinking off to the bog AGAIN to avoid buying a round. So on your way back you greedy bastard, don't come back without three pints in your grubby little Fagin fingerless gloved hands. One for you, and two for me since I have bought the last two rounds, oh yes, and I'll have a bag of nuts as well.

Ian never changes and never stops trying it on and pleading poverty. It was always the same at school; Ian could peel an orange in his pocket and could smell a Mars bar being unwrapped whilst scrounging a drag on someone else's fag in the school bogs. And would you believe it, he's back from the bogs with two halves and he's conveniently forgot my fucking peanuts and he has that pathetic old codger absent-minded look on his face that fools nobody.
"What's this?" I shout at him as he plants a half of bitter in front of me, "And where's me nuts ya' greedy bastard?"
"Don't be like Tez," he answers all old, sad and forlorn, "You know I've got a bad memory and I'm a poor man. You couldn't lend me fifty quid whilst I get my memory back could you Dave?"
I just shake my head; the greedy sod never stops trying it on.

It is not a widely known fact but under his alias of Ian Achmed as he used to be called in his boyhood days, Ian has a very famous Arab heritage. He is in fact half Arabic, Yemeni to be exact and now keeps it quiet by changing his name to Ian Newton. In fact, when the British museum was excavating an ancient site in Arabia, they discovered an ancient betting shop and one of Ian Achmed's ancestors was encrypted in an ancient nearby tomb. It was thought the tomb went back to before BC times. It was documented as the first ever ancient Arabic suicide to be discovered. Apparently this ancient mummy relative of Ian Newton's (Alias Ian Achmed) was found with the fist of its right hand tightly closed with a look of horror on its face. So tightly was the fist of mummy closed that it took tomb excavators the use of a crow bar to prise open the ancient hand. And when they finally got it open, there was a folded up note inside the hand. Carefully they opened the note and it said, "Four million pounds.... to win......Goliath!!!" And that was the start of the Achmed's family climb to success across the centuries until they finally made it to the shores of England's green and pleasant land on a night darkened beach of Dover UK, having sneaked into the country on the back of Ox cart returning from Calais – nothing changes that much does it.

Yes, the Achmed tribe arrived on our good shores, broke and without a penny to scratch their arse with after the bottom fell out of the Camel trading business in Yemen. And then of course there were the rumours, that the family had been run out of Yemen for trying to fix the annual Arabic Camel Racing Grand National. Only rumours mind you......(Touché!!!! You bastard – rent arrears and rabbits under the sink eh?)

Sorry to interrupt you Terry in the full throws of your introduction to the readers, it's Ian Newton here. I can't let you get away with that slander on the honour of my family's good name, especially in camel racing circles.

Just a minute Tez, that's libel that is, you can't write that, I'll have you in court if you had any money. I'll damn well make you bankrupt Sir for that slander...Oh I forgot you already are bankrupt. And what about your ancient family history, yes you're keeping that one a big secret ain't you Coxy. Well if you won't tell it I will. There was a story on Hessle Road that one of your ancestors was the last person King Harold spoke to at The Battle of Hastings in 1066. King Harold was reported as saying, "Hey Coxy you idiot stop messing about with that bow and arrow, you'll have someone's eye out."

Sorry about that rude interruption readers. This is Terry Cox back again and Ian has just bolted for the door as an angry female face from the past spotted him and started shouting and ranting something about unpaid maintenance, with the caveat, "You bastard!!!"

Right now Ian has done a runner and I don't think, with fat Mavis pursuing him at some speed of knots it is likely we will not be interrupted again, so here's my grumpy pitch and small rant at the world for what it's worth.

The people, events and stories are true you are about to read in this shinning example of working class literature at its best. And you get them delivered in these pages' warts and all. Since we are going to pull no punches about ourselves, we see no reason to let other folks off the hook.

To those who did not live through our times of 1950s, 1960s and early 1970s, you accepted life as it came at you, and every body talked plainly and called a spade a spade. If someone did not like because of your colour, your weight, your appearance or whatever, you more often than not got called names. If it was you that got picked on or bullied, you were forced to stick up for yourself and had a fight and either you beat them up or they beat you up, but either way, win or lose, a point was made and consequences shown. It was just the way it was, basically dog eat dog. And dare complain to your parents that someone had called you a name or hit you and the answer would be usually, a big thump around the head and the harsh words of parental wisdom, "Well hit them back then and keep hitting them back until you win."

So, it was face up to your enemies or run and hide, and you look around today at this risk averse country of ours and see children forced to wear safety goggles in the playground to play conkers and you despair and wonder what our country is coming to. God knows what we will ever do if Britain ever has to face the Russians on the battlefield. No doubt we will send in an elite battalion of "Health and Safety" officers in pink tanks to take them on with some "Rupert" the tank commander popping up out the turret to do a risk assessment and giving some Russian "Boris" soldier a piece of his mind, with words like, "Put that bloody bayonet down Luv before you hurt some body." And I joke not, and I think all those of you out there from my generation will know absolutely what I mean.

Sad to say, our once great country, is one big mad house nut job and many of us feel like we are living down the rabbit hole in Alice in Wonderland. I am worse than Ian when it comes to ranting about politics, but enough said but, "Where is Guy Fawkes when you need him?"

But enough of the rantings of two old farts and let's get on with the story after I've thrown in my two penny worth. So here goes.

If you are easily offended by foul language, sex or vulgarity, then this book is not for you. But don't be so hasty, you never know, it just might be, and you never know what you will enjoy until you've tried it, as I used to tell an old girlfriend who had never tried the doggy position. So I'll hope you'll buy it as me and Ian need the money as I suspect Ian is down to his last hundred thousand.

But I have to say that we do live in strange times and today's society seems to have gone mad and people of our age seem to be constantly being hit over the head with a shitty stick by the so-called P.C. Brigade and I think sometimes, they would rather we went away and died off quickly, after of course ensuring we have paid our due taxes. Though they might not know, our generation has a name for the PC brigade and we know them simply as SPLACs (SAD PEOPLE LOOKING FOR A CAUSE). They have no sense of humour and maybe that is why their sole purpose in life seems to be to meet once a month in a dimly lit cupboard under the stairs, plotting new ways to make the world a more sterile place and devoid of humor mainly because they have never had humour or known real working class laughter, or any sort of fun in their sad lives. My own opinion is, that when we stop laughing at each other, we soon start shooting at each other. At the moment, like Ian I feel like a stranger in my own country.

No, this book is for the countless thousands and tens of millions of people brought up in hardships the 1950s and 1960s. - The POST WAR GENERATION. Like me and that tight old git Ian, they yearn for and want a nostalgic trip down memory lane. They were brought up on the bawdy humour of Steptoe and Son, On The Buses, and other later sit-com greats such as Rising Damp. Oh God where did those years go? Such bloody good days.

I refuse to change the reality of my childhood to accommodate those who see my life and the life of many like me as an inconvenient truth or a history those in the PC Brigade regard as now inappropriate. I refuse to change the truth and apart from tinkering with some of the bad and the sad bits, the answer is no.

In today's nut case society if you gave a child a plank of wood today and a few nuts and bolts and a pair of pram wheels to make what we, in my child hood days called a bogie, the SPLACs would be all over you like a like a bad dose of knob pox, mumbling about Health and Safety and the need for a risk assessment. In our day everything was a game with few holds barred because we learned to amuse ourselves as that was all we had; a sense of adventure, inventiveness and a great desire for mischief and fun. I look back at this once great country and I could almost cry. The war generation rebuilt a great nation for their post war children and now the lot is just being given away wholesale. God what a terrible inheritance we are leaving our children and grand children. Just listen to me, I'm ranting again, I just can't help it. I'm getting as bad as Ian. And what do you know, Ian is back and "Where did you get that black eye?" Looks like fat Mavis caught up with him.

Now I have to explain a point of controversy here about writing this book with my long time buddy and former Hessle Road Gas meter raider, Ian Newton (alias Ian Achmed, Police record Number 25476) and that is this. How do two people write a book together? I mean how do readers know who is writing what part of the book. Now Ian, the dodgy bastard, has graciously said he will do the writing and I will provide some of the funnies, and he adds, with an odd glint in his eye, "Don't worry Tez, I will make sure you get your money, you leave the money side to me, let me worry about. We go back a long way me and you Tez. Hessle Road buddies don't ripp each other off, do they Tez. You can trust me....old mate!"

Yes, I know what you are thinking readers, TRUST!!! Ian Newton!!! The dodgiest bastard north of the Himalayas. Just a minute, let me look in the mirror and see if I've got "Silly Bastard" written on my forehead.

So anyway after much civilized negotiation and a tight squeeze of Ian's nuts and he begins to see the issues from my perspective. And it is agreed we write the book this way. Wherever Ian is writing a part of the book, it will say, "Ian Newton" is writing that particular part, and where I am writing a part of the book it will say Terry Cox is writing that part of the book. That way we can see who gets the most laughs. We have also agreed to open a secret joint Swiss numbered bank account to pay in the royalty dosh. That way all them thieves at tax office will have to get some other suckers to pay for those piss-taking MPs fiddling their expenses, oh yes and those other thieving bastards in the "EUSSR"

Surprise, surprise Ian has agreed and I have stop squeezing his balls and we shake hands on the deal. I count my fingers and that my watch and rings are still there and the deal is done.

So, anyway all rants and disagreements over, and to all those out there like us, get out the Pale Ale, get your lass a Cherry B or a Babycham, sit back and laugh your bollocks off. You ladies can find something else to laugh off as you join the Hessle Road Scallywags on another tour down memory lane with us to once again meet the characters that lived down Marmaduke Street and up and around the Hessle Road of the 1950s onwards.

Chapter One

Marmaduke Street, The Street of Misfits

Fate is a strange thing and I suppose, like God as they say, it works in mysterious ways. I hadn't seen my old childhood best mate, Terry Cox for more than 40 years. After leaving our factory fodder school we all just drifted apart. It's not something you mean to do, it just happens. After we had both left Boulevard High School in west Hull, or as we called it in those days, The Four B's, "Boulevard Borstal for Backward Bastards". Independence Day came for us "inmates" on a sunny June day in 1970, and when that final bell tolled for the last week of the very last day of our 5-year senior incarceration, there were few teachers left manning the establishment and for their own safety they had scattered and retreated to a locked staff room.

It was always the same when the senior year was leaving school for the last time. We were big boys now and many with hard Hessle Road reputations that went with it and some of us leaving that day carried scores that needed settling. Often in past years the final day had been marked with classroom riots, scuffles and punch-ups breaking out all over the school, as pupils picked fights with both teachers and other pupils known for being teacher pets and informers to settle long festering grudges as canings, sometimes brutal canings, were routine in those days, and the last day of term was seen as pay back time for many a good beating that had been inflicted on many.

As was usual in the final week threats of vengeance had been abound, as were rumours of what teachers and their pupil pets were going to cop it big time, and in past years some teachers had been given a pasting as accounts were duly settled. And anticipating trouble by the time it came for us to vacate the school premises for the last time, the school had almost been surrounded by a small army of coppers and we, the final leaving year were escorted off the premises by a waiting Police honour guard to ensure not only the safety of the teachers but that the school building wasn't burnt down as so many pupil-teacher grudges seemed to get settled on the very last day of term. And so fresh, youthful and full of bravado we marched out the classroom like a marauding horde of Viking savages signing at the top of our voices in a loud chorus of rebellion, the traditional Hessle Road School leaving battle cry of,

'BUILD A BONFIRE, BUILD A BONFIRE, PUT THE TEACHERS ON THE TOP, PUT COPPERS IN THE MIDDLE AND WE'LL BURN THE FUCKING LOT!"

And so we had finally left school, yes the day you thought would never come had actually arrived. It was an unreal day; our life sentence was really over. We were really free, no more fucking school, no more fucking teachers ordering and pushing you around. We were free to go where wished and stay in bed till sunset if we wanted without constantly being harassed by that legendary schoolboys' scourge and general pain in arse, Mr Key, or as we nicknamed him after the famous Hessle Road Butcher's shop by the same name, Ted Key, the School Board man.

If you have ever watched the American Western TV series, GUNSMOKE with the "hard knock" fast gun U.S. Marshall, Matt Dillion, well Ted Key was his equivalent as he rode the streets of Hull and Hessle Road on his trusty steed, a pop, pop moped tracking down school truants and those absent without leave, as it were. Ted Key treat his job like a holy mission and would hunt down truants and school absentees with all the determination and tenacity of a Pinkerton Detective Agency bounty hunter chasing Butch Cassidy and The Sundance Kid. Old Ted Key even wore, the same type khaki gabardine overcoat and Trilby hat as a Pinkerton Bounty Hunter, only the trustee steed was replaced with Ted's equally trustee moped and you could not miss his ominous figure coming down the road a mile away as the pop, pop, pop of his moped would be a dead give away and you would all scatter in different directions. And for some reason Ted always chose me to home in on and he would spend the day chasing kids up and down all over Hessle Road playing cat and mouse until he had got his man. No, Ted Key the school board man never gave up once he had you in his sights and he always got his man. But in them days I was a bit of a dodgy little bastard and was one of the few that gave him a constant run for money, and many a morning old Ted Key had come bounding into my house without so much as a by your leave, stomp up the "apples and pairs" like he owned the place, and my Mam would stand there without a care in the world, propped up leaning carelessly against the staircase downstairs puffing on a Woodbine, and rejoin up the stairs, "Cup of tea Mr Key?" whilst Ted Key bodily dragged me out of my warm cozy pit on a cold Winter's mornings, drag me down stairs in my underpants and threw my clothes on the floor and shout so loud it was almost like the wolf in Red Riding Hood, "I'll huff and I'll puff and blow your house down," and my old lady would puff some more on her woodbine hanging out the corner of her mouth and make Ted Key a cup of tea like they were old friends and say, "I don't know Mr Key I can't do 'owt with him, the lazy little bastard just won't get out of his pit."

And so old man Ted Key coming crashing in on my bedroom became something of a regular Monday to Friday morning routine for me. You would think an innocent little boy like me could have some sanctuary in his own stinking little pit knocking out Z's but it was not be, and if that was not good enough for old Ted Key he would then pace me on his moped all the way to school whilst easily puffing away on pipe like a railway steam engine as he shadowed me all the way to school gates like a boxing trainer following and pushing his quarry to exhaustion. "Come on Achmed," he would shout as he rode just along side me, "get those knees up lad and let's see you get a spurt on I haven't got all day. When I was 17 years old I was carrying a fifty-pound back pack and a Lee Enfield rifle, dodging Krout bullets on the beeches of Dunkirk. The army lad, that's what you need, they'd make a man of you, you lazy little tinker. NOW MOVE!!!" And my little legs would be going ten to the dozen and I would reach the school gates, sweating and panting like an exhausted greyhound, and just to be sure I didn't get lost on my short journey to the class room, Ted Key would frog march me up to the class by the scruff of my neck, open the class room door and chuck me in with the same rejoin of good bye, "See you in the morning Achmed!!" And so the saga of my constant battle with Ted Key the school board man would go on for many years.

And I very reluctantly admit it, I was a little dodgy bastard when I was a kid and often I had no trouble conning the teachers on this or that, and played many of like a piano, but Ted Key, I don't think I ever got one over him once. And even when me and Tez dreamt up this really good con for twagging school, Ted Key was all over us like a bad rash. We had this idea. In the mornings we all went to our form room to get a ten-minute attendance register called and then went to other classrooms for this subject or that subject. So we worked out, we could just go in for the register and when we went to other classrooms, we would just skip out of school. But alas one day after register had been called, about five of us were piling out the school gates, and suddenly a voice called out, "Hello lads. And just where do you think you are off to?" We all looked round in horror and there was Ted Key, leaning against the school wall puffing on his pipe, and the game was up and after a good canning of six of the best on each hand by the head master, the school register was sent to every classroom whenever we changed classrooms and that closed yet another escape route to skipping school. Yes, old Ted Key was a real pain in arse but I did have my victories against him and so did Tez, but they were few and far between. He was one wily old fox, I'll give him that.

But now it was all over, I could do what I liked, I was free, we were all free, and no more Ted Key. Unlike Terry who could get up in the morning, I liked my pit far too much and even Terry trying to knock me up in the morning for school was a wasted cause because as he was banging on the door and shouting through the letter box, I was in the land of nod contentedly knocking out the Z's all snoozed up and dead to the cold world outside. Yes, Old Ted Key did seem to have it in for me and did his level best to make a model pupil out of me. But despite his best efforts even Ted Key failed miserably and his lack of success in getting me to school regularly was a real blot on his copy book of successes and a big downer for his reputation of always getting his man.

And yes, whilst Ted Key did on many occasions chase me down and foist me off to school, in the end vengeance was mine. And now, I would like to make an admission to Ted Key who should now be about 120 years old, and the mysterious case of his missing moped. Yes, Ted, twas we, me and Tez who nicked your trustee rusty old steed, and since Boulevard High School was sea going school, renowned for producing the hardest sea going rascals and trawling Fisher Kid pirates let's make it a nautical sounding confession.

"It be now me hearties 47 year since that old varmint Ted Key's moped be purloined from outside of the school boiler house and was sent to the bottom of Davy Jones locker with a gurgle and to a watery grave in the grey murky depths of the Humber." But before we nicked Ted's mobey, what Ted Key didn't know is, that as he supped his tea and and sampled the delights of a morning bread and dripping sandwich as he sat listening to the morning groans of desperate Hessle Road Mums with twagging kids. We usually had mischievious plans of our own for a snatched ride on Ted's mobey whilst he was otherwise engaged socializing. So let's just call this dark dastardly deed, "THE LEGENDARY SCHOOL BOARDMAN INCIDENT," which would go down in Hessle Road folklore for many years to come as the revenge of the Hessle Road Scallywags. And we hope you wont think too badly of us, but old Ted Key from our point of view, did get his comeuppance that day.

So this day me and Tez and another kid, to be introduced in later pages, known as Ugly Plug was twagging with us when we heard the distinctive sound of the pop, pop, pop of Ted Key's mobey, which sounded like a fart in an echo chamber and we knew Ted

Key was on the prowl for truants. Like the wind we legged it to the nearest alley hide-out just as Ted Key rode by puffing on his pipe. For the hell of the chase to come, we pushed Plug out the alley, and me and Tez shouted, "TOSSER!" up the street to Ted Key. And as quick as a flash, the would-be Texas Ranger, Ted Key, pulled on the reigns of his trustee motorized steed leaving it abandoned in the street and legged it like the wind to hunt down Plug, with his belted mucky gabardine mack flying about in the breeze and holding onto his tribly, he chased Plug down relentlessly to round him up like, the cowboy Rowdy Yates rounding up a loose steer in Rawhide and pursued him into the next street – "Herd 'em up, move 'em out."

Me and Tez looked at each other and laughed, our luck was in as we saw Marshall Ted Key's mortorized mount abandoned and untethered. It was a chance too good miss, and I jumped on Ted's fart box and it was "Hey yo Silver away," as the Lone Ranger would cry. But I soon found out I was riding a wild mustang and this nutty little kid soon lost control and I was heading straight for The Milky Bar Kid's front door and unable to stop what happened next and with a loud thud I buried Ted's mobey straight into the front door before legging it back down the alley with Tez following quickly behind me. There are couple of grown up chararcters in this scenario, like The Milky Kid and Workshy Cyril that will be described in later chapters, but they were street characters unique to the times and we had a lot of fun with them down our street as you will read later. But a brief desciption of both theses characters are that the Milky Bar Kid as we nicknamed him, was just one of few street drunks and work was a four-letter word to him. He was as bog eyed as a bag of welks and rarely sober. As for Work Shy Cyril he also spent most his time stagerring out the local pub having spent his day and his sick money getting blottowed usually after being kicked out the local betting shop. Both lived next door to each other in their shitty little hovel two-up-two down houses, know as Corporation Houses because the local City Council owned them.

Anyway, no sooner had we fled the crime scene after putting Ted Key's moped through the front door, before The Milky Bar Kid emerged through the debris, still half cut from the night before and scratching is head, wondering where the fuck the moped stuck in his door came from.

Now in moments like this, misunderstanding tend to arise and just as Milky Bar was inspecting the felonious, malicious damage to his "estate", Marshall Ted Key comes moseying round the corner and he suspiciously eyes The Milky Bar Kid, and as the two men suspiciously eyeball each other, you can almost hear the sound of Mexican Trumpets heralding from the last showdown scene from THE GOOD, THE BAD AND THE UGLY- and in this developing scenario we can deduce that the Milky Bar Kid takes the role of THE UGLY. And suddenly Marshall Ted Key and The Milky Bar Kid face each other down and in slow silence stalk each other as behind the twitchy curtains the good "law" abiding citizens of Marmaduke Street hide in terror as showdown approaches. And as Ted and Milky Bar slowly shuffle towards show down, you almost hear someone whistling, "Do not forsake me oh my darling," from the film, High Noon and for the purposes of what is to follow we cast Ted Key in the "goody role" of Gary Cooper, as he suspects The Milky Bar Kid of trying to rustle his trustee, rusting steed, and now the dye of showdown is cast, as Milky Bar also suspects Marshall Ted Key of shooting up his front door.

Now me and Tez having caused all the mischief, and watching it pan out with great expectations from behind the safety of nearby wall giggling away, you would think this scenario couldn't get any more complicated, but unfortunately it does and it would seem that Workshy Cyril having risen from his pit has his own bone to chew with Milky Bar over a hot dead racing certainty Milky Bar had tipped Cyril with a nod and a wink the day before and the whispered words, "It can't lose Cyril, put your shirt on it." But significantly, it did as Milky Bar was about to find out with the gravest consequences as Cyril approached rolling up one sleeve and clenching his fist. This was getting better by the moment, "I want a word wiv, you, ya bog eyed bastard," Cyril shouts shooting from the hip, "That fucking hot tip horse you gave me, is still running." And without a further a do, Cyril donks Milky Bar a big one right in the mush and it's "Timber!" and for Milky Bar it's, "Adeous Amego!" as the lights go out.

Now if there's one thing you can say about Hessle Road Fish wives, they do get stuck in, and Mrs "Milky Bar Kid" seeing the love her life being assaulted by the local Saddle Tramp she was on Cyril like a wild alley cat and armed to the "one black tooth" with a big dirty dustbin lid she let fly at Cyril, but being as bog eyed as her old man Milky Bar and Cyril seeing it coming, he quickly ducked only for Marshall Ted Key to get it right in the kisser with a big metallic keplonk and Ted Key hit the dust.

Feeling smug and satisfied and with a good day's mischief done, and having got vengeance over Marshall Ted Key, we rode out of town into the Sunset and, "did one" before the pose arrived.

It was just one of the many memories of fun and mischief that came our way in our childhood days as me and Tez walked home in a dizzy haze full of ourselves and could hardly believe, school was at last over. We were all full of youthful bravado and brazenly lighting cigarettes and puffing them off in the faces of the teachers and the coppers as we taunted them on our march to freedom. And out of the rowdy crowds some of us couldn't resist throwing the occasional brick and putting a few school windows in as a parting shot as a token of our last goodbye and fucking good riddance.

Whatever we thought of that last day at school, I think few of us really had any idea of the big bad world to come and how hard it would be for many us. And in later years we would all come to realize that wise truth the teachers always quoted at us with that wry smile of their own worldly experience, "When you're older, you will all look back and realize your school days, were the best days of life, and you will regret wasting them." But we were young and who listens when you are young, full of hell and full of the arrogance of what you think of is eternal youth. I don't think there is one person in the world that doesn't get to me and Terry's age and say, "Why didn't I listen when I was young." Or "If only I could go back in time and know what I know now." Oh yes, with age comes great experience and wisdom, and great regret at the waste. Me and Tez have no doubts that today's youngsters will get to our age and have the greatest of all regrets of any generation in the history of the United Kingdom. But let's not go there.

At that moment in time, whilst we might have thought our friendships would last forever, the ever-turbulent rough seas of life would simply sweep us up in its ripe tide and carry us wherever it chose. I don't think when me and Terry walked out to freedom through those school gates all those years ago that anything would break the friendship that had bonded our little gang together for so many childhood years of mischief. But times moved on, and slowly but surely the lives of all us separated as me and Terry came to that invisible fork in the road and we both toddled off on our start down life's long tortuous and often cruel highway in different directions and for many years, "Never the Twain shall meet".

I had gone off on my life's long journey of travels and a thousand jobs and so had Terry. He had done his time at sea on trawlers and then transferred to a life as Jolly Jack Tar the Ocean Pig and gone Big Boating in the merchant navy for a life on the ocean waves and travelled to too many countries to mention and steadily gone up the promotions ladder to Boson. And so in over forty years our 'ships' of life had only crossed in the night and never docked in the same port, if you will forgive the seafaring metaphor. Life does that to you, it just takes you in different directions and eventually, without even noticing the whispering drift of time and years have moved on and you lose touch, and those most precious of all friends, your childhood friends have fizzled, faded and suddenly disappeared from your life and they become no more than occasional memories you look back on in your later years, and maybe smile or laugh at as you remember some of the mischief and fun and maybe you wonder where those days and friends have gone.

I will though mention here a little amusing footnote about a minor detour Terry took in his sea faring career and that he spent some time in, and wait for this because it's not a wind up. Terry actually spent some time as a Rod Stewart lookalike and earned quite a few bob at it, appearing at posh parties and weddings and once when flying out of Heathrow Airport to meet a ship, and who should be waiting in the bar lounge but Rod Stewart himself. And Rod Stewart called Terry over and accused him of taking the piss but in a joke. I have to admit that in those days Terry was a dead ringer for Rod Stewart and of course had his hair done like him. Apparently Rod Stewart thought it highly amusing and bought the whole crew a drink. Then of course there was the added benefit on his trips across the seven seas that many a girl in foreign ports were left laid blissfully in the bedroom somewhere, in the mistaken belief they had spent the night shagging Rod Stewart. But alas time has moved on and Terry not having anywhere near the coin of Rod Stewart could not hold back the aging process as Rod Stewart has with some expensive hocus pocus elixir of youth and the plastic surgion's knife. So now Terry has given up the Rod Stewart lookalike game, but is now a real dead ringer for Worzel Gummage.

To tell you the truth I haven't bumped into many of my childhood friends from Hessle Road, as after the slum clearance of the area many of us were scattered across the city to the four winds. And I think I would have had some difficulty in recognizing some of them now. But sometimes someone does pass you in the street or the town centre and you get a pinprick in your mind, as the ghost of a vaguely familiar face hidden behind the aged mask of time floats past you, and you both momentarily glimpse at each other, but are unsure whether to say hello you just walk on. I must admit whilst time is hardly kind to any of us, I have bumped into some childhood friends and passed them thinking, "Fucking Hell he must have had a hard life." And who knows he may have been thinking the same about me. I am not one for relighting old fires and such things as face-book has yet to entrap me with any fascination and it's not something I use, or have an attraction to or ever likely to.

But with my old mate Tez Cox I didn't have any problems in recognizing him, or him me as we passed each other in St Stephen's Shopping Centre in Hull. We both instantly stopped in our tracks, looked at each other and just burst out laughing without even exchanging a word. And you know what, both of us knew exactly what we were laughing at. It was our time as children living down Marmaduke Street on Hessle Road. That's what Hessle Road does to you, it gave us both unforgettable memories imprinted into our very bones, and as best childhood friends in extreme mischief making, our histories bonded us like Red Indian blood brothers.

I suppose it was also the "black and white" times we lived in, times of struggle, family hardship and the comings and goings in all hours of the day and night of a sea faring community. A knock at the front door and taxi driver standing there outside, and it was, a kit bag over the shoulder job and your big brother or Dad was gone. Yes, it was a strange, fast living time of faces just coming and going in the fleeting transience of the moment. And seemingly for us children with so much endlessly going on around us we just got on with our mischief, fun and street games totally oblivious of the slow but sure creep of changing times gathering around us, and how it would move us on along the road of life's journey without us even noticing it.

Everybody seemed to be in rush in those days; everybody seemed so busy just getting on with his or her life's struggles and battles. For many, especially the Fisher Kids it was a time of, live for today and fuck tomorrow because we might not be here. There always seemed to be party time on Hessle Road and after the pubs called chucking out time at 11pm, the drinking, wives or girlfriends moved on homeward and Fisher Kid parties seemed to go on every night, somewhere in some street in the little two-up-two-down houses spread across Hessle Road that were usually filled with brand spanking new on-tick furniture. And with what always seemed to be a padded mini cocktail bar and the record player a must-have in the posh parlour to blast out at full volume the latest hit records into the early hours. And us kids would stay up late and hang around outside the partying houses and had a little party of our own, and sometimes local school aged lasses would bop the night away outside on the pavement, and it would not be long before half the street was partying as the booze from inside the house drifted outside the house and into the street. Yes, there was many a midnight conga train jigging from end of the street to the other into the early hours.

There would also be plenty party poopers and you could guarantee that some miserable old Scrooge-faced git who had to get up in the morning would start moaning, and bedroom windows would slide up and angry abuse would get shouted into the night as someone would blast out angrily at the tope of his voice, "DO YOU KNOW WHAT TIME IT IS! I have to get up in the morning, turn that fucking noise down!" And that was how many a blood and snot punch up started and both me and Terry remembered some epic drunken street scraps as the fast living partying Fisher Kids did battle with the street landlubbers.

Even though many of us children had little in the way of money or material stuff and many had bad home lives, we would find our own escape and seek our own refuge and steal some of the partying fun off others just enjoying their time and their moment. And then of course there where the girls, how could you forget the girls because you would always get a good soggy snog or maybe a bit more before the party faded. And then as ten or maybe twelve trawlers went out the next day with an equal numbers coming in, and it would all start all over again as every night became Saturday night across both Hessle Road and Hull with taxis buzzing around like busy bees carting their drunken cargo of Fisher Kids up and down Hessle Road and across town to fill themselves up to the gunnels with booze for a one way trip to alcoholic oblivion for three days and three nights and then back to the ship sober or drunk.

Me and Terry must have been stood laughing and talking for more than two hours in St Stephen's Shopping Centre that day, with passing people looking at us like we were nut cases as we loudly exchanged memories and laughter at the mischief and mayhem we wrought on Marmaduke Street and remembered some of the solid gold characters that lived down there. In many ways Marmaduke Street was a street of more than its fair share of misfits and such strange, colourful and unique characters like you could not believe lived there and helped make our time a fun one and they gave us as good as we gave them.

Tez had read my book Hessle Road Scallywags and said he almost cried with laughter as he recalled some of the characters and some of our wild, sometimes out-of-control antics we got up to. He made the admission that I heard from several other friends from Hessle Road, "You bastard," he said with a laugh, "I always wanted to write Hessle Road Scallywags, and you beat me to it." And here I reminded Terry of one night of particular mischief and four of us, Me (Then called Ian Achmed) Terry Cox, Jimmy 'Isse' Turner and Frank Callis, sat on the doorstep of a corner shop down Marmaduke Street in the early morning dark hours, laughing at some mischief just carried out and one of us had said, I think it was Terry himself, "Ya know, when we grow up, one of us should write a book about Marmaduke Street."
And Terry just looked at me startled and said, "You know I remember that and I always thought about it, but never got round to it, and you beat me to it."

He also said there had been a frenetic round of telephone calls and gossip going around about the Hessle Road Scallywags book, with lots of family and friends saying how they howled when they read it and copies were being circulated bountifully. "What did you tell them about that girl in the cemetery for?" Tez said at me with a big belly laugh, "My sister Linda rang me up, saying what a dirty little bugger I was. And you forgot to mention that Ernie was with us that night." And Terry was right, I had totally forgotten that another old friend Ernie was with us on that lost night of brief passion in Division Road cemetery all those years ago. If present readers are wondering what we are talking about, you will have to read the book Hessle Road Scallywags. But we all sort of lost our virginity that night, or at least we think we did.

I had thought that I had burnt out all my memories of mischief and fun from my childhood Hessle Road days, but it was only after bumping into Terry that I realized how many characters I had forgotten about and how many more incidents of both innocent and dodgy mischief we had actually got up to. And both of us found ourselves creased up in the middle of St Stephen's shopping Centre in Hull, as we reminded each other of what little bastards we were.

And there was no two ways about it, we were little bastards, but ours was in search of fun and mischief, and of course the odd bit of business to make a little money, by hook or by crook. And certainly there were many others on Hessle Road who did far worse and not in the name fun but vindictiveness, and that was never our motive. In those days there seemed to be no constraints on us, and so we took the piss as much as we could and also on occasions took the consequences that might be in the form of a good hiding or a chase from some grown ups we regularly upset. But that was the whole point of our mischief making, it was the fear and fun of the chase that made our mischief all the more exciting and it just became addictive for our little gang.

Chapter Two
The misfits

Well by the time we had finished talking, we both knew there was another book to write about The Hessle Road Scallywags and so me and Terry decided we would write it together. A week later and we get together on a Wednesday afternoon in The Avenue Pub down Chanterlands Avenue in Hull with pens and paper at the ready and the pints of Tetley's best bitter beer lined up like regimented soldiers, and so we began.

"You forgot so many characters Ian," said Terry looking at his notes. All the previous weekend Terry had racked his brains and made a list of characters and incidents I had totally forgotten about and so began our regular weekly drunken jolly jaunts of mischief down memory lane and it wasn't long before we were in alcohol driven stitches of laughter ourselves on too regular basis, and we laughed more and more, as you do when the beer flows and helps loosen up the imagination and inhibitions.

Yes we have been getting a bit pissed too regularly lately I have to admit on our afternoons forays slinging together Hessle Road Scally 3 much to both our lasses remonstrations of, "Are you pissed again?" our lass would blast at me falling in the door with all the clumsiness and verbal diarrhea of W.C. Fields, "What you see before you my dear, is not drink but alcoholic induced happiness!" I would sarcastically blast back as I staggered in. "We've just oiled the wheels of literary imagination to loosen us up and get the creative juices of humor and composition genius flowing." I would spout as I tried badly to pretend to be sober. And yes, our lass was right I was pissed and so was Terry and his partner Jane gave Terry just as much earache.

But if there was one thing that the years hadn't changed about Terry, it was his sense of humour, and just like mine, it was still as stupid and as childish as ever. Terry had made somewhat of a comprehensive list of all the diamond characters and misfits that lived down our street and locally that, we as extremely mischievous kids made a hobby of winding up and playing the most outrageous tricks on. So let's get this story going and introduce some of those characters that Terry reminded me of and that we will weave into our story as we go. I think it might be prudent here if we also rehash descriptions of the characters already described in the book Hessle Road Scallywags as we might have new readers going straight into this book. And so we have to appologise a little to those who have read the first Hessle Road Scallywags for this rehash. So let's do the introductions and have some fun as we go back to the Hessle Road and Hull of the 1960s.

"Taffy Touchwood" was one of the oddest characters that lived down our street and was called so because he had this really strange habit of touching and kissing telegraph poles and trees and it had been known on more darker nights, and eye witnesses reported that his distinctive night blackened skinny silhouette had been seen prancing about in the twilight morning hours like a Victorian cloaked phantom seeking urgent sexual gratification by rubbing himself up in a frenzy against anything wooden and upright that was in the vicinity and bolting into the night as horror filled female screams echoed the lonely streets. Yes, Taffy Touchwood had struck again. And the word would go out that Taffy Touchwood was on the prowl, and just like the eerie Hessle Road legend of 'One Armed Nellie' old Taffy had disappeared like a puff of smoke, his despicable urges satisfied and his dastardly deed now done. Yes, trees or telegraph poles, nothing was safe from nefarious sexual assault when Taffy Touchwood was on the loose in the silent hours. Even though Taffy Touchwood was an oddity no one took him that seriously, though I am sure not many women would have enjoyed bumping into him on a black windy winter's night with the night blackened trees of The Boulevard rustling in the breeze when Taffy Touchwood was on the razzle with a bulging full sack that needed emptying. But whilst old man Touchwood's antics might have scared hags, girls and old bags loitering around in the dark hours in search of trade, if you know what I mean, he never really scared us kids and in strange sort of way to us he was just part of the overall tapestry of weirdness that was I suppose normal down our nutty street. It was just a weird street full of really weird characters and whilst they were weird they weren't dangerous or anything, but they were bloody good fun for us kids.

Now "Plug" was another character and nicknamed so because of his striking resemblance to the Beano comic strip character in the Bash Street Kids, though the comic cartoon character was far better looking than our Marmaduke Street version, so that's saying something and gives you an indication of how ugly our Plug was, yes he was one ugly fucker. He was also about six feet tall and as skinny as a trimmed up malnourished bean pole, so much so that a hearty blast from a well aimed sloppy fart would have blown him over and Plug was forever trying to throw his height about with other kids. Whilst his size might have looked intimating, all the local kids knew Plug could not knock the skin off a cold rice pudding on a good day. And the outcome was always so interminably predictable and, just like watching Batman and Robin, after quick, "Wham" and a "POW!" it was over before it had started and as ever Plug would drop like a sack of nutty slack being thrown off Black Joe's coal lorry after the first punch had been thrown no matter who he challenged. No, poor old Plug never learned his lesson, and once even the local street 'bike', so-called because she gave all the local boys a regular 'ride' if you get my meaning. Yes, Polo was some what of a naughty little local Nimpho but never went all the way if you know what I mean and for some reason bothered me quite a lot for a snog and some hot pressing on her parents' couch, that did us both the world of good. But apart from that I certainly came away from many a night baby sitting with her more than satisfied because after starting with the snogging she would dry hump you to death and at 12 years' old that was as close as many of us youngsters got to actual slam dunk sex if you get my meaning.

As I have said, Polo seemed to have the hots for me, and whilst I tried desperately to resist Polo in case my Mam found out, I just couldn't help myself and who could, when a girl is continually flashing her knickers at you like a spider to the fly. But I suppose I was as bad as Polo and who could blame her because down Marmaduke Street there wasn't much in the way of good sex for girls unless of course you had brothers in the family.

Anyway Polo was this little skinny lass's nickname, so nicknamed for reasons I will leave to your imagination, and she downed Plug with one big donk right on the snozzler when he had tried to ambush her in the dark in a nearby derelict bombed out house in the hope of releasing his perverted lustful intentions in her knickers.

Now Polo had developed this sort of obsession with me, and told everybody she was my girlfriend and going out with me. Going out with someone in those days meant you were their boyfriend. Although I kept telling Polo I wasn't her boyfriend, I can see how she got the wrong idea, because we did spend an awful lot of time, I am ashamed to say, snogging and hot pressing each other on the couch when she was baby sitting. I suppose it was because she wasn't much to look at that always put me off being seen in the street with her. And whilst she wasn't much to look at, she had this one hell of a little hot nubile body and always when our paths crossed, she would look at me with this wanton face of like girly lust. And if I resisted she would get out the big guns and play real dirty, and give me a quick glimps of her skimpy school girl knickers and say all cheeky and suggestive, "I'm Baby sitting tonight Ian," then look at me with this sultry face and ooze at me, "I'll be waiting Ian," and just by the way of some more torture she would again flip up the front of her school gym slip and give me another flash of her knickers and of the possibilities on offer, "See you later then Ian," and she would walk away grinning, leaving this little confused and frustrated little boy standing in the road with eyes open wide and urges going through his body that he did not quite understand. And however determined I was to resist Polo's offer, I would find myself slowly gravitating my way up the streets, and one way or another, me and Polo would end up on the couch snogging the socks off each, and pressing ourselves over each other like randy rabbits on a spring morning, until that point of pleasurable oddness was reached and the urgings were suddenly gone. And I would slink off into the darkness feeling thouroughly ashamed of myself for once again falling for the temptress charms of Polo and of course what me Mam would do to me if she found out.

But it would seem that even the ever lusting Polo had standards she would not sink to and she drew the line at the thought of showing her draws so Plug could vent off the throbbing loins bulging in his skiddy stained grey under kegs. Yes, poor old Plug had certainly drawn the fucking plug ugly card in the baby looks lottery, and had alas not been endowed by nature with any of the attractions that qualified you to get your leg over with the local lasses in Constable Street School playground on a dark Winter's night as many did, in those long gone halcyon days of rolling thunder and hot "wham bang" teenage sex that frequented nightly those much loved school playgrounds.

There is a rather ironic foot note to the story of my and Polo's on/off childhood snogging sessions, and this happened some years later after we had all gone our separate ways as it were. I was about seventeen years old I think and at the Mecca ballroom one Friday night. There was this stunning sexy hot girl just oozing sex appeal across the dance floor, and like all arrogant sods at that time I mentally marked her out for a smooch, a snog and a pelvic press when a slow record came on. So just as the music started, like grease lightening and with a throbbing pouch, I bolted across when the next record came on before anybody else could move in, and as you did in those days, I just tapped her one the shoulder, and you always got a dance at least. And yes, suddenly I get a mental slap in the face, and you've guessed, it was Polo. Talk about the ugly duckling, Polo had bloomed and SHE WAS FUCKING GEORGIOUS with these long legs that went on forever. And arrogantly thinking she would still have the hots for me, and all over flowing with confidence I was getting her into bed that night, I walked up asked her to dance and she smiled at me all arrogant and gave me the bums rush. And I was left standing in the middle of the dance floor looking like a right dip stick. Yes,

Polo didn't love me anymore it seemed, and I suppose it was poetic justice considering how I treated her when I was younger.

Chapter Three.

Other characters were, and we as kids had nicknames for them all, "The Milky Bar Kid" who was as bog eyed as a bag of whelks and actually looked like that old silent movie comedian Ben Turpin and could be just as funny as him as well but not intentionally, it was just the way The Milky Bar Kid was. He was so bog eyed and always so pissed up he needed a map and compass to find his front door and when he was telling you off you were never quite sure who he was talking to.

"Yes I'm talking to you, ya' cheeky bastard," and he would stand there drunkenly swaying and pointing at some body but looking at somebody else. "Anymore of your cheek and you'll feel the sharp end of my boot right up your fucking arse."

"You touch him and our kid 'ell kill ya'!!" someone would shout.

"Fucking bring him then," Milky Bar would shout back, "and I'll do him as well." And he would do this little shadow-boxing dance in front of us like it was a threat, "You fuckin' bring your kid then," he would brag at us as he bobbed and weaved around the pavement, "I'll give him the old one-two, and the bastard won't know what fuckin' hit him. I'm hard I am, fuckin' hard."

And a taunting big "Ooohhhhh" would go up from the crowd of kids surrounding him and Milky Bar would turn and stagger off down the street having giving us what he though was a good old gob full. "Fuckin' cheeky bastard kids," he would mutter, "I've fuckin' shit, em." And then he would stagger up the street cursing and swaying and suddenly stop dead in his tracks, his expressions would go all blank and vacant as the booze got the better of him and he would keel over like the proverbial sack of shit and hit the deck and lay there in a crumbled scruffy heap until his misses came out and picked him up. And as she did, in chorus we would all sing in a loud cheeky chorus at them, "THE MILKY BAR KID IS STRONG AND TOUGH AND ONLY THE BEST IS GOOD ENOUGH. THE GOOD TASTE THAT'S IN MILKY BAR...THE MILKY BARS ARE ON ME!!!!!!"

"Get home ya' cheeky little bastard's!!" Missis Milky Bar would shout at us as she dragged him up the street by the scruff of his jacket like he was the overflowing dustbin that had fallen over. "Go wash ya fuckin' knickers Missis we can smell 'em from here," someone would shout.

Funnily enough The Milky Bar Kid we all thought was a fitting nick name because the only soap he ever saw was Coronation Street and many a time he had been chucked out of Criterion Pub at the corner of Marmaduke Street because he would just stink the place out. Not that that was unusual, as quite a lot of people who lived down Marmaduke Street seemed to react to soap and water like Count Dracula did in the late night movie to having Holy water thrown at him. Yes, there were a lot of real fucking stinkers down Marmaduke Street there was no denying that. The Milky Bar Kid was married to who we called Mrs Milky Bar Kid and just like her husband if she had had a good wash she would have lost about three stone and the rumour was that when she did venture a bath they put the Humber Mud dredgers on stand by otherwise there would have been another sand bank blocking the River Humber

I mean don't get me wrong, lots of people down Marmaduke were mucky bastards, it just went with the territory and even many of us kids spent our days covered in dirt and grime from many a day rummaging through derelict and partially demolished houses for stuff to nick, rip out and flog. And sometimes we would give the demolition man some out of hours help by pulling down the old houses ourselves.

Once the demolition men had gone home we would scramble about all the derilict house looking for where the demolition men had hidden all their gear. They were never very good at hiding it and we would climb over all the piles of half demolished house carrying sledge hammers, ropes and pick axes we could hardly lift and have a go ourselves. We just wanted to see something go TIMBER and fall over in a cloud of dust.

Next thing you know and me and Tez and usually Isse Turner and Frankie were climbing all over half demolished houses tying off ropes around walls. And once we'd set up we would all heave like hell on the rope that we had tied around a half standing house wall and it would, slowly at first, just start to sway as we pulled and then suddenly come down with a big cry of "Timber" and a big shit dust clouds would suddenly explode over us and engulf us and we would emerge through the dust coughing and sluttering as the walls came down in a crash and we would get covered up to the gunnels in grime, soot and dust from head to foot. And if it defied our efforts to pull it down we would usually burn it down, and as the derelict house was reduced to ashes we would all sit round the smoking embers till gone midnight roasting potatoes in the red hot ashes just like it was Bonfire Night and down Hessle Road during the slum clearance it was Bonfire Night almost every night for us kids during the slum clearance.

So even we rarely looked scrubbed up except when once a week the old tin bath came off the backyard wall and you would all be shunted through the same bath water in age order with the eldest going first, and so since I was the youngest in our mob, that meant usually stepping into a mud bath after following the previous three into the same bath water. And I have some sympathy for Terry because he was the second to youngest in a massive family of brothers and sisters, so he got a right bum deal on bath night.

But Mr and Mrs Milky Bar Kid gave being a mucky bastard a whole new meaning and turned it almost an art form. We never saw the Milky Bar Kid in all our years down Marmaduke street ever wear anything but this what must have been this second hand ex Fisher Kid ice blue suite that over the years had become so filthy and engrained with booze, food and rings of piss stains around the rusty zip area of the trousers. And his arse trousers were so shiny with wear you could have used his backside as mirror, but few would want to get that close to his arse. It was often said by many down Maramaduke Street, that if the Milky Bar Kid ever took that suite off, it would walk to Criterion Pub all by itself.

Mrs Milky Bar like a lot of women in those days would often sit out in the street on a sunny day showing off her "corn beef" ringed legs, a testament to too often roasting herself against a hot coal fire on a cold night as she warmed up the delights of her fulsome body for a night's passion with any passing dodderer hard up enough to bang on her drum to slip her one whilst Milky Bar snoozed off his days boozing on the couch.

It was like a street ritual and she would sit with her legs wide open getting some well needed air to her muff, as we used to say. And like many street hags in those days, they all had this odd habit of sitting out on sunny day with legs spread akimbo with muffs and dirty gussets en mass staring at any passing innocents and you could not help getting eyeful of what looked like a dirty, hairy furry dead fox nestled between their legs. Oh no it was not a pretty sight by any means and enough to put you off shagging for life but as the saying goes, "a stiff prick has no conscience" and gossip had it around the street that many of the local shag-deprived scruffs had been poking Mrs Milky Bar for years behind Mr Milky Bar Kid's back and one of her regulars was "Work Shy Cyril"

And 'Workshy Cyril' is the next actor to be called up to our historical stage of real life comedy and poverty to take a bow and to continue the sorry saga and ongoing litany of the dramas of the drunken, hapless and luckless inhabitants that lived down our street, and immortalized at that time, by being given the unwanted title of being, the dirtiest and muckyest street in Hull and also renowned as, the Marmaduke Street of freaks.

Yes, just in the middle of Marmaduke Street lived or existed might be a better word, "Work Shy Cyril" and his legendary glass back, that didn't seem to give him much trouble when he was endlessly banging Mrs Milky Bar when the Milky Bar Kid was three sheets to the wind, and as pissed as the proverbial fart sprawled spark out on the pavement outside the Criterion after one of his many epic boozing sessions on dole day.

When Cyril wasn't sampling the forbidden delights inside of Mrs Milky Bar's smelly, rarely washed Boyes bloomers, Cyril could be found eagerly trying to make his fortune in the Bookies on the corner of Cholmley Street and Constable Street screaming like a crazy man at the frenzied horse racing commentary blasting out the radio on the bookies wall. As kids me and Tez were often stood outside of the bookies trying to get some of the grown ups going in to put a bet on for us, and you could hear Cyril screaming his head off like he was coming in his trousers as he tried to push his horse to the winning post, "GO ON!!! GO ON YA BASTARD!!!!" Cyril would scream at the radio, as others around him would scream just as frenzied for their horse, until the noise of shouting and screaming came to an out-of-control crescendo as the horses came to the final furlong, and suddenly the voices would die into a big deflated groan of disappointment as their nags lost. And the only certain bet was on Cyril usually losing everything and his shirt, if they would have took it, which was very unlikely. And all hunched up, forlorn and totally deflated Cyril would emerge all sullen and cursing and angrily rip up his betting slip to shreds and amble down the street, hands in pockets and often stopping to head-but a nearby wall in self chastisement, whilst screaming those immortal words over and over again in blasting self criticism as he gave the wall another pasting with his head, "Silly bastard!! Silly bastard!! What are you, a fucking silly bastard!" As again he'd run at the wall and nut it.

Oh yes, Cyril always had a hot tip burning a hole in his pocket, but alas, if there was ever a born loser, it was "Work Shy Cyril" and he couldn't back a winner in a one horse race. And as they say today about winning the National lottery, you have more chance of being struck by lightening twice than getting six little numbers, and given hapless Cyril's luck, you could guarantee, that if he'd have won the lottery today, as soon as he had picked up the cheque, he would have been struck by lightening as soon as he had picked it up. Yes, poor old Cyril's regular flirtations with Lady

Luck was definitely unrequited and after an afternoon's session having filled the bookies cash register with his sick money, cursing and mumbling like a crazy man and with only shrapnel left in his pockets, he would burn it down to the local and drown his sorrows scrounging pints or mine sweeping beer in Criterion pub till chucking out time. And then spend the rest of the night keeping the street awake nose-to-nose rowing in the Terrace at the top of his voice with his long suffering super fat misses, "Mouldy Mavis" on the pavement outside the house, with as they say, the air turning blue in a no holds barred slagging match that always turned into a slugging match as "Mouldy Mavis" planted a couple of big ones right on drunken Cyril's mush.

"You fuckin' lazy drunken bastard!! You've spent all the dole money again!!!" and as pissed up Cyril goes down from Mavis's lightening right, and up comes her foot with the speed of Bruce Lee as she rags around a drunken Cyril and she almost lifts Cyril off the ground as her boot meets his bollocks and Cyril curls up like baby on the pavement as Mavis's boots fly in from every angle. Old Cyril is get a real pasting and a crowd has gathered and bedroom windows are up with heads rubber necking and egging Mavis on. A mob of us kids have gathered in a circle around Mavis shouting in a frenzied chorus, clapping and stamping our feet, "Fight!! Fight!! Fight!!" And egging her on to plant a few more on Cyril.

The centre of life down Marmaduke Street was the pub on the corner of the street, The Criterion and it must have took a fortune in dole and sick money and you could often see Work Shy Cyril fall out the door, swaggering and swaying off down the street singing to himself without a care in the world. And the next day, usually at dinner time he would emerge onto his door step in his mucky grey string vest with trousers that looked like he had slept in them, because he probably had and he would stretch himself, lift his leg, let out a splashy fart and take in the world around like a Texan rancher surveying his acres and the conversation with The Milky Bar Kid opposite would always start up the same. Cyril would cough his lungs up and scrape the back of his throat and

spit out a great big green one, start rolling a fag and say to Milky
Bar, "God I've just been shitting through the eye of needle. I tell ya
Les, it was coming out pure bitter, pure Hull Brewery bitter Les.
Ya could've put a pint pot under my arse and it would have had a
head on it." Just in case you're wondering, Les was The Milky
Kid's real name, or at least the one he used for signing on with.

So as the sun rises and Work shy Cyril is up and out of his flea pit,
it's the start of just another normal day down Marmaduke Street,
and for the moment time for us to leave Cyril and The Milky Bar
Kid in the throws of neighborly banter and move on to some more
sterling characters that made Marmaduke Street known as the
Legendary, STREET OF FREAKS. But don't be down hearted there
will be lots more shit and snot flying in the pages to come.

Now I have to warn you here, in those days down Hessle Road no
one took any prisoners when it came to name calling, taking piss
or whatever. And if you were black skinned, brown skinned, wore
glasses, were fat, bald headed, a smelly or scruffy bastard or even
if you had a physical affliction, it mattered not, you got a nick
name and you were fair game for having the piss taken out of you.
It was nothing personal; it was just the way things were. So don't
judge us lest you be judged as the saying goes. But I don't
remember as many people as today getting murdered or girls
raped in my childhood days and the streets were relatively safe
for children. Now that is in stark contrast to today where the
political pundits of today will condemn as savage and
inappropriate the days of my childhood, whilst now living
through the most immoral and crime ridden times I can ever
remember, and whilst there were plenty of drunken punch ups
and rows galore in our street, we just survived.
As a half-caste kid, I got called a black bastard, wog or nigger
many times and usually you had a fight and sorted it out and it
was the same for all us kids. It was just the way it was and those
who lived through those times will think nothing as they read on,
but of course there will be those who will read on and be totally
outraged, but do you want the truth or lies? So let's say it how it

was and get on with meeting more of the characters from our street in 1960s and leave the PC Gestapo to live in their own alternative reality of hypocrisy.

Now "Clumper" was the nickname us kids had for this old smelly bloke who had one massive foot much bigger than the other and who used to sell Hull Daily Mails from a vending stall in town and would push his rusty old Hull Daily Mail bike with a basket on the front, from town all the way down Hessle Road to our street where he lived. In those days nearly everybody bought the Hull Daily Mail because it was a real big newspaper in those days not like today and had a dual use, and after you had spent the night reading it, you spent the rest of the week wiping your arse on it and the black print would stain your underpants along with the brown skiddies, except that was on a Saturday when you could get the green coloured Hull Daily Mail Sports Edition that was not much better for wiping your arse on, but at least the colour change, as make shift bog roll, wouldn't stain you under kegs so much.

Hull Daily Mail vendors used to act like Town Criers in those days, and they would shout out what they were selling, and the headlines on the newspapers, like, "Bent Labour Councillor gets prison for double glazing scam!" to passing people, but what used to come out of their mouths was the most amazing and funny gibberish that bore no resemblance to the name of The Hull Daily Mail they were flogging, like "Smmmmail!!!" one would cry at the top of his voice. All the Hull Daily Mail street vendors had their own individual cry and it was like their signature song. Our man Clumber would have a unique street cry of his own selling The Hull Daily Mail and his garbled sales pitch cry would come out something like this "Castashoosmmmmail!!! GET YOUR Castashoosmmmmail!!!!" I mean how the bloody hell did that sound like "Hull Daily Mail?"

So for us kids there were lots of scope to take the piss big time as the Hull Daily Mail vendors stood shouting and plying their trade and we kids would stand next to them mocking their cry in their efforts to flog the Hull Daily Mail and it wouldn't be long before we would piss them off and they were chasing us through town, and if they caught you, you would get a good hiding. We were always talking the piss out of Clumper as he pushed his bike home down Hessle Road after a hard day flogging his newspapers. Clumper always came plodding down the road about 10 o'clock at night and we would always ask him the time because he would repeat it over and over again.

"Hey Clumper," we would shout at him, 'what time is it?"

And Clumper would rejoin squawking in this high pitched voice like a parrot repeating over and over again as he plodded off in the distance, "It's about ten, about ten, yes it's about ten, about ten, about ten, yes it's definitely about ten, ten o'clock that is, definitely about ten o'clock."

This one night Clumper must have got a bit arsed off with us nightly taking the piss out of him, and one night as we started up our routine and Clumper suddenly turned us. It was a fucking ambush and old Clumper had a pre-prepared pile of newly pulled up grass clods in his bike basket and suddenly he started pelting them at us and two smacked me and Terry right in our mush and we were covered in muck and soil dust from head to foot and I could smell dog shit in my hair. "Fuckin' right!" and we all looked at each other, ran across the road, pulled some grass sods and returned fire at Clumper covering him in soil just like he had done to us. But unfortunately our aim was not that true and one of the grass sods missed Clumper and went speeding through the open door of the fish shop and smashed against the counter showering a queue of people in the fish shop in shit, grass and soil, and out piled a crowd and the chase was on. And when they caught up with us we got a real pasting and I had a black eye for weeks, Terry got a fat lip and cauliflower ear, but did we complain? Did we fuck because we would have got a bigger pasting from the coppers or our Mams if we had gone to them. No the coppers or parents never had much sympathy for us little scruffs in those days, and so we dusted ourselves down and called it quits with Clumper and lived to fight another day.

Hessle Road in them days was so full of 24 gold Karat characters like you would not believe. I suppose they were what was called in those days, the locals nutters, and just like most of us scruffs, fate had landed them on the very bottom rung of the poverty ladder of life scratching a meager living on some bread line hand to mouth job or more usually a career dolie or on the sick. Today you don't get characters like that walking the streets of Hull as most of them would be probably get locked up or elected to Parliament or become local councillors.

When I think back it was weird really and Terry thinks the same on this one, we don't know why Hessle Road in 1960s had so many odd bods walking the streets but we did, so let's not get distracted with social analysis and get on with introducing a few more of Hessle Roads characters and apologies for slipping in such words as "social analysis" but me and Tez can't resist showing off sometimes and showing that our vocabulary does stretch beyond "Fuck off and Bastard".

So quickly moving on then, some of the characters you saw and some you could just hear coming through the throng of Saturday shoppers getting in the bully beef for the once weekly Sunday's roast belly busting blow out before it was back to eggs and chips or dripping and dry bread for the rest of the week.

Yes, it was the distant whistling that always gave this unique character away, and sure enough there he came moseying down the road like one of those cowboys off Rawhide with, as always one hand seemingly glued into arse back pocket and with his back all hunched up. And it could only be one person, that confused fashion icon of the 1960s, "Let's hear it folks for, the one and only Mr Ducky Drake," my mate Terry would announce in a piss taking mocking trumpet fanfare as Ducky came skating up to us sporting the latest in five- bob Boyes's store Tec Sack jeans with turn-ups up to knees (he wasted nothing) and looking like he ironed his vest over a wok and forgot to take it out. I bet you're thinking his nick name was "Ducky" because his surname was "Drake" but you would be totally wrong, Ducky was his real first name, and you had to wonder what half-wits of parents would name their kid Ducky with a surname of Drake, but they did. Now Ducky had this almost strange and unique way of walking and it seemed to defy the Laws of physics, but somehow Ducky just did it. He'd walk like he was on skates, but move as slow as a tortoise, and would like slide his feet forward without lifting them, similar to Michael Jackson's moonwalk but going forward. And sometimes when our little gang would pass him in the street, we would sneak up behind him in a long line and all put our hand in our back pockets and as quietly as we could just follow him in a long line with all the Saturday shoppers looking and laughing at us imitating Ducky's walk and then as he whistled we would join in whistling and suddenly he knew we were behind him and he would turn round chase us and give us a gob full.

"Ya cheeky little bastard's!!" he'd shout up the road at us, "I'm telling you lot, you'll feel my belt when I get my hands on ya! Don't worry I know where ya' live."

"Come on then Ducky you old bastard!" we would all shout back piss taking and old Ducky would take his belt off wave it in the air and chase us up Hessle Road shouting and screaming with the air full of "Fucks!!" "Little Bastards!!" and "I'll fucking kill ya!!" I don't know whether Ducky had memory problems but the next day he would just walk past us on the road as though nothing happened, even sometimes smile like a gormless monkey and it would all start up again in the same old routine.

The odd thing about Ducky was that although he walked so slowly, he seemed to pop up everywhere just walking and you would see him in the town, in East Hull, down Beverley Road, he seemed to get everywhere, and there he was, just walking and whistling, hand as ever in his arse hole pocket, oblivious to the world and just cruising through life without a care in the world.

Even though our gang of me and Terry, Frank and Jimmy were still only about twelve or thirteen we rarely went home until the early hours and would often hang about the street talking and plotting mischief late into the night.

Being twelve or thirteen is a difficult time with such things as girls. I mean we all knew there was a reason to like girls, but we were at the age were it was still considered 'soppy' to be seen with a girl and seen kissing them even soppier. But one girl did tend to hang about on the fringes of the gang, and was forever trying to get me to snog her. Yes, I'm talking about Polo. As I said she wasn't much to look at, but she always seemed to sneak up on me at weak moments. And when I say weak moments, I was at the age when looking at girls gave you that odd tickly feeling in an odd sort of place. And Polo could be a bit of a little boy's temptress and she had this strange power over me, and often passing her house, she would appear on the doorstep in her short gymslip, pout her lips and say all tempting, "Ian, me Mam and Dad's gone out, we can watch Thunderbirds together." And even though I knew what this would lead to, I just couldn't help myself. And if nobody was looking, I would whip into her house with rising excitement I didn't understand, and my arse was no sooner sat in front of the telly, and, "THUNDERBIRDS ARE GO!" and Polo would dive on me squelching her wet sticky lips all over me, with her ragging and pressing on me like a girl possessed by a little demon. Now I'm not saying it wasn't enjoyable, for a reason I didn't understand at that time, but I always felt so guilty afterwards, and wondered what me Mam would say of she found out. I mean all we used to do was snog and have like these pressing on each other sessions, and I didn't know why at the time, but the pressing on each other sessions seemed to do the trick, if you know what I mean, and this odd urge in a certain part of my anatomy would suddenly disappear in an explosion of "Fireworks" for both me and Polo, and I would always promise myself it would never happen again, but of course it always did. And Polo just had this power over me and she knew all she had to do was give me a little glimpse of her knickers and I was under her spell for another snogging and pressing session and after, as usual feeling ashamed and guilty, I would slink quitely out of her back way hoping nobody would spot me and guess what me and Polo had been up to. Yes, when it came to me and Polo and these 'pressing' sessions, there was no controlling ourselves, and afterwards we would lay on the floor panting and out of breath. And once as I lay there staring up at the ceiling with the fires of teenage urgency having been put out I said, "Why do we keep doing this Polo?" And she would smile all cheeky and girly, "cause it's nice though in't it Ian." And I couldn't argue with that. "If me Mam finds out, she'll kill me." I said a little panicky. And I would get up and leave, determined never to return.

Some times if the gang was planning to stay out late, we would all scour our pockets and put all our loose pennies and six pences together and buy a cheap bottle plonk and five park drive tipped from Bev's off licence after getting a grown up to go in for us. And we would sit on the steps of a derelict shop at the end of Marmaduke street, and slowly get pissed and generally making a nuisance of ourselves, knocking on peoples' doors and running away. One night we decided to booby trap Stuttering Joe's front door. He was a local misery guts that hated kids playing outside of his. But oddly never minded the young lasses playing double ball against his wall with their school gymslips tucked into their blue serge school knickers. Mmmm I wonder why?
Anyway this night all revved up with cheap plonk and full of mischief we nicked a dustbin lid, got some rope and Tez borrowed his Dad's ladders from the garden shed. And under the cover of darkness, me, Tez, Frank and Isse snook like commandos down a sleepy Marmaduke Street. Now some people will remember that many front doors had like a little roof facade outside. So we quietly put the ladder up against Stuttering Joe's front door, tied the rope to the dustbin lid and put the dustbin lid on the little roof over hanging Joe's front door. And then tied the rope to the front door handle. Now Stuttering Joe was getting wise to kids playing "knock off Ginger" on his front door. "Knock off Ginger" was the name given by the kids to the game of knocking on doors and running away. Anyway Joe had wised up to the midnight knock at his door, and was usually out as fast as a bolt of grease lightening so he could belt the kids outside with a big slap across the lug hole and swing a solid boot up your arse for your trouble. But we had

a plan to deploy counter measures and once all was set, we retreated to a nearby back alley some distance away and threw two half bricks at his front door that landed on his door like two loud knocks. Well no sooner had the bricks hit his front door and Stuttering Joe pelts out the front door like a mad man possessed and spitting fire, "Gotcha! ya little Bastards!" but instead of getting his hands around necks of the kids he thinks are banging his door, he walks straight into the dustbin lid that falls off the roof and with a great big loud donk, it smacks him right on the nut and the lid then crashes to the ground with a big loud metallic rattle and roll that echoes down the street and bedroom lights are going on and windows are sliding up.

And they see Stuttering Joe laid out cold in a heap on the pavement and cries of abuse echoes around the street, "Is that you Joe?" the neighbours are shouting. "Do you know what time it is? I've got to be up in the morning." And another shouting, "It's fucking Stuttering Joe, the lazy bastard is pissed again and laid out cold! I'm gonna come down there and do you." And another shouting, "Never mind spending all ya dole money in the pub, try cleaning ya' house ya' mucky bastard!" And the windows slam down and the lights go out and silence descends across Marmaduke Streets as Stuttering Joe slumbers under the stars.

I don't suppose the people and kids would have antagonized Stuttering Joe as much but he was such a trouble causer, always cuffing kids across the lughole and spreading gossip. Mind in those days gossip was just a way of life and what wasn't true was just made up. So there was always lots of stand up toe-to-toe blazing rows in the streets that usually ended up in a wild west punch with all the fish wives out on their doorsteps with curlers in and their factory turbens still on giving it loads. And enjoying every minute of the rumours being spread about, true or not, as it would give them something to gas about about for weeks.

And what was really funny to listen to was when people were rowing in the street and going at it hammer and tongs, you could always bet, that all family skeletons in the cupboard would be shouted at each other. "Oh yes Mavis!! Well you want to watch ya old man, he's been dipping his wick with her down Walcott Street. He can't keep his cock in his pants your Bert!" And the air would turn blue as they pushed and jostled each other in the middle of the street. It was just the way it was in those days, but you could bet in the coming days, that all would be forgotten and they would all end up having a drunken sing song in Criterion come the next Friday night and they were all back buddies until the next time.

But whilst down Marmaduke Street we did fight and row with each other, in a strange way we all stuck together as well when it came to outsiders causing trouble down the street. And usually then every body was out and piling into the outsiders. It was very territorial in those days and you tended to stick to your own street and venturing out of your area usually meant you got filled in by the local street gang who didn't like you in their street. Coppers especially were not welcome down our streets and as soon as a cop car appeared, a big group of nosy gossiping neighbours and kids would congregate to find out what was going. And one night there was this cop car parked outside of Stuttering Joe's because he'd clouted one of the local kids and the cops had been called. As a baying crowd gathered outside Joe's house and were shouting for his blood, the coppers came out of his house and cleared away the crowds, "Now get off home or we'll arrest the lot of ya'!" and gradually the crowd slowly and grudgingly dispersed and the coppers disappeared back into Joe's but not before one of the lads had tied a rope to the back axel of the cop car and tied the other end to the lamppost outside of Stuttering Joe's house and as the copper came out and got into the cop car and sped away, suddenly there was a loud crash as the coppers pulled down the lamppost and it keeled over and crashed through Stuttering Joe's front door. Poor old Stuttering never had much luck with his front door after the legendary incident when Radish had demolished it when he crashed his motor bike into the same said lamppost and ended up flying over the handle bars and head butting Stuttering Joe's front door. It was Terry who remembered the incident with the cop car.

Chapter Four

Now to cast your mind back to the book Hessle Road Scallywags, you may recall to memory that on Hessle Road in those days, those rumoured to partake in nefarious twilight sexually activity with animals of the canine species were known to the locals as a PUDDING HEAD. So once again, those who have read Hessle Road Scallywags will, I am certain remember Peter Pudding Head. And Pete Pudding Head you rarely saw during day, and like many down Marmaduke street, sinister stories were abounding about Pudding Head and his nocturnal sexual activates with his trusty canine on the bombed out waste ground at the bottom of Marmaduke Street. And once you got a name for something down Marmaduke Street, guilty or innocent, it mattered not, it was usually impossible to get rid of it and you were stuck with it for the rest of your days, with kids and grown ups alike taunting you morning, noon and night. Me and Tez are thinking here it might help here if we gave you a rehash description of what Pudding Head looked like and we will do our level best to conjure a detailed, comprehensive, unbiased and fair picture of him that will help you allude in your mind's imagination what this major protagonist in our story looked like. Now both me and Tez want to be balanced in our description of Pudding Head and we don't want you to think that we are in any way trying to set you against Pudding Head just because he was an alleged, and we stress the word alleged, because nothing was ever proved, a "Midger" as well as a Pudding Head, and we will elaborate shortly what exactly a "Midger" is, so don't worry on that score eager readers. But be restrained a moment, as me and my mate Tez wish to give Pudding Head the benefits of the doubt being the good fellows we are. In our book, a man is innocent until proven guilty and we have to hold fast to those hallowed principle of English law that men over the centuries and histories have fought and died for on the field of battle and that led to the signing of that historical document The Magna Carta at Runnymede in 1215. Yes, we must hold fast to justice, Liberty, Fraternity and Equality when giving fair judgment on Pudding Head. So holding fast to, and bearing in mind these hallowed principles we will begin our description of Monsieur Peter Pudding Head appertaining to the year of our Lord 1967.

You might think this is a hard start of our description but we are actually pulling our punches here but, Pudding Head was one hell of mucky looking and smelly bastard and with his thick sinister bottle lens glasses and black and yellowing full set of tombstone nashers, he just looked the part of classic sex perv. But on the mucky bastard side of things, he was one hell of a stinker. But that in itself was nothing odd for Marmaduke Street, as most of us were all mucky looking bastards at the best of times. But at least us kids would try and would get a bath at least once a week and at a push once a month whether we needed it or not.

But not Pudding Head, when it came to soap and water Pudding Head was a highly principled conscientious objector. Though giving Pudding Head his due, it had been said down the street that the last time Pudding Head had taken a bath was for the street party in 1945 for V.E. day and even that day was not marked without serious incident according to local street historian, hag and gossip "Nimphy Nora" also nicknamed, THE FISHERMAN'S FRIEND but the nickname was nothing to do with the famous mint lozenge of the same name I can assure you of that, wink, wink, nudge, nudge, "Say no more".

Nimphy Nora swore blind on a stack of bibles, and crossed her heart and hope to die, even to this day that Pudding Head had taken advantage of Sweaty Betty, who having succumbed to over exuberance in celebrating Britain's moment of victory over the Krouts, and also having partaken of far too much Hull Brewery mild, had flaked out and she had graciously been helped back to her house by Pudding Head. And all that was known and reported later was that Sweaty Betty had been found out cold, bent over the back yard washing mangle, her big fat bare arse in the air, with her surgical stockings and bloomers around her ankles having been given a good old Hessle Road humping dogey style. And whilst nothing was ever proved or the evil culprit found, the blame as to the identity of the mystery abuser who had taken advantage of a pissed up and defenseless Sweaty Betty that day, had fallen on numero Uno suspecto, as they say in Spanish, Peter Pudding Head.

Now me and Terry are not taking sides on this one and we will have to leave it for history to judge if it was Pudding Head that had indeed been the dastardly perpetrator that had given Sweaty Betty the alleged good reverse poke that day over the said alleged washing mangle, in the vicinity of her own backyard.

Now all down the street had been aware that Pudding Head and Sweaty Betty had been teenage sweet hearts at one time or another and that Pudding head had jilted her at the alter at the last minute after he discovered that the local coalman had been banging her for years behind his back. And whilst Betty claimed it had been nothing more than an impetuous fling in a mad moment of Hull Brewery fuelled lust, it did not explain why Pudding Head had caught the dustman climbing out of her bedroom window in his underpants or the ragman, oh yes and the postman and the window cleaner. And after much thought and soul searching, he felt sure Sweaty Betty could not be trusted with his love.

And sadly Pudding Head may have been right on that one as rumour had it in fact that many others down our street had partaken of Sweaty Betty's well hidden sexual delights. And she had been spotted many a time falling out the door of the Criterion Pub accompanied by three dark and dusty mysterious seafarers, and they all ducked into a nearby alley for a quick knee trembler, with all us kids gathered at the entrance eagerly trying to get a gander of what was going on, and got an eyeful as Sweaty Betty took one at the front door and one slipping her crippler at the back door whilst the third was on the hand pump. Yes, Sweaty Betty was certainly mult-skilled in the shag department. Yes, when me and Tez thought back, there seemed to be awful lot of illicit shagging and extra-marital bonking going on all over up and down Hessle Road in those days. And they shagged all over the place, down alleys, on wasteland, graveyards were always a popular spot. And of course us kids being curious, we would always sneak up and watch and wonder what was going on with all the grunting and groaning coming out of dark places. In fact, it was the only sex education we got in those days. And whilst we might have been curious little kids, it never stopped us bringing out the old catapult, loading it with a big fuck off staple and firing in a broadside as we would all let loose down the dark alley ways and run like fuck as screams of agony echoed from the darkness as our barrage hit home.

But getting back to the burning question as to who had reverse rogered Sweaty Betty over the mangle on that fateful day in 1945. Me and Tez knew who our money was on. Whilst me and Tez are pointing the finger at no one as to the V.E. day culprit who took advantage of a pissed up Sweaty Betty and left her flat out drunk and battered and bruised bent over that washing mangle. Though it would be fair and reasonable to say, many, many had passed down Sweaty Betty's Grand Canyon before. But what we would say further, is that this alleged incident did add to Pudding Head's historical reputation in the street and made many females in the street wary of his presence in the haunting dark hours when the sinister black silhouette of Pudding Head could be seen walking and exercising his canine beast around the lonely ways of Marmaduke Street in the satanic dark hours after Midnight.

As for Sweaty Betty, it was said she never got over the trauma and developed an obsessive fear of men and washing mangles. And only a few days after the terrible incident, had been compelled to give the washing mangle to the local ragman for two bob and four balloons, two blue and two red. Yes, that washing mangle had to go, as it bore too many painful memories of V.E. day 1945. And it would be many days before Sweaty Betty could face returning to her regular therapeutic evening jolly jaunts along the dark foggy docks puffing on a Capstan full strength, in her red mini skirt, and her elephant legs wrapped in red patent leather thigh length high heeled pirate boots and swinging her matching red paten leather handbag in gay abandon to all those friendly, smiling foreign seaman, who often out of common courtesy and good manners would regularly offer Sweaty Betty a warming cup of tea on board. Yes, Sweaty Betty was a Mission to Deep Sea Seaman all on her own and she had a real "soft spot" for the sea faring man and it was this love and respect for the well being of United Nations of seaman that she paid tribute to the bravery of these "men in peril on the sea" by honouring them by naming her children after a few of them, Abdul, Vladimir, Helmut and the youngest Sirius. Naming the youngest after the ship as it was much easier.

I can see here that me and Tez have become somewhat distracted with Sweaty Betty and neglected to finish the low down on Pudding Head and his laxity in the soap and water department and other serious matters alleged against him.
With Pudding Head, it was his extreme lack of personal hygiene that usually meant you could smell him coming some distance away long before you saw him, especially if the wind was blowing your way. Yes, you could have easily have been fooled that sewers were blocked when Pudding Head was prowling about, but no, the stink would usually be Pudding head stepping out of the front door of his two-up two-down shit hole of a house where it was said Pudding Head lived with his old mother. Although no one had ever seen Pudding Head's mother for years, the neighbours swore blind they could hear them talking through the walls on a night, and many comparisons were made with Pudding Head being another Norman Bates nut job and that his mother's dead body was probably sat up in her bedroom in a rocking chair with Pudding Head prancing about the house in his mother's clothes swishing about a six inch carving knife. But as I say that's only speculation and we don't want to let our imagination running away with itself.

But of course us kids couldn't resist winding up Old Man Foxy who lived next door to Pudding Head with all the latest rumours on Pudding Head. And one day as Foxy was waddling along the street pushing his rusty old pram down the terrace, in his black trilby hat with a feather sticking out of it, a gypsy muffler tied round his neck and sporting his iconic dirt sodden black overcoat that was about two sizes too big for him, laden down with his latest bargain basement purchases from Gilbert Baitson's auction rooms, plus a broken television.

Foxy had this unhealthy obsession with old televisions and always bought second hand tellys, working or not, he always had one tied on top of his pram as he pushed it down the street. And when I say unhealthy obsession with old tellys, it usually turned out unhealthy for both buyer and seller of one of Foxy's tellys, as the tellys had this habit of blowing up and injuring the purchaser who would then seeks purchasher redress by punching Foxy's lights out.

Old man Foxy would spend his days in what he called his "workshop". And like some mad Professor Quatermass Foxy would spend his evenings sat in his front room that was packed wall to wall with old tellys and old side board size radiograms busily beavering away with his head stuck in the back of a stripped down telly dangerously poking and prodding the electrical guts of wires and valves in the naive and very dangerous self belief that he knew what he was doing. Some times Old Man Foxy would strike what he thought was gold, and after a lucky prod and twist here and there, he would step back to a safe distance and turn the telly on, and voila, it would work. But the big question would be, for how long? More often than not soon after Foxy had got a telly working he would bolt to the local shop before it stopped working and put note in the window, "TELLY FOR SALE, IMMACULATE. ONE OWNER. 30 Bob and it's yours!!!"

Now few could afford their own telly in those days and if you had one, it was usually one of those big clumsy Redifusion monsters that was the size of an old sideboard with a tiny black and white screen. They usually had these dirty big channel changing knobs on the side that you needed the strength of Hercules to switch TV channels with as it clunked from channel to channel, the total number of channels in those days being two and three channels if you were lucky and had BBC2. And for BBC2 and the Friday night Midnight movie there was a special button you would have to push in with a big thud and you could watch, The Wolf Man,

Frankenstein, Dracula and The Mummy. And if you were baby sitting with a bird on a Friday, they would get scared to death and cuddle up to you on couch. Most tellys in those days were on "the never, never" as credit was called in those, or they had this big one-shilling box meter on the side that you fed with shilling pieces so you could watch the telly on a sort of pay-as-you-go. I suppose it was an early 1960s version of pay-per-view. And once a week the Redifusion man would come round to empty it, that is if you hadn't robbed it, or your next door neighbour hadn't. Yes, a lot of people in those days robbed their telly meters, gas and electric meters and tried to claim somebody had broken in.

So as you can see every one wanted a telly in those days and even new ones were always breaking down. And Foxy of course being ever the entrepreneur, being it flogging chickens or "mending" old tellys, he never missed the chance to make a bob or two. Well as the saying goes, there's one born every minute and since tellys were so expensive in those days, that thirty bob might seem a bargain, for a day or two anyway. Until of course the inevitable happened and Foxy electronics genius ended up blowing up in your living room or bursting into flames as TV game show host, Michael Miles was about to introduce, Tonight's Star Prize on Take Your Pick.

Yes, sad to say Old Man Foxy didn't have many satisfied customers, or healthy ones either for that matter after they bought one of his televisions de pierce de resistance. And as the fates would have it, many a purchase of Old Man Foxy's electrical goods ended up in tears, a big loud puff of blue smoke and a near death experience.

You always knew when Foxy had flogged one of his dodgy tellys to some unsuspecting thick Hessle Road Palooka, because as soon as the hot dosh was in his grubby little mits, it was straight down to the Criterion and he would spend the night pouring Hull Brewery mild down his neck until chucking out time, and spend the next day being chased all over Hessle Road by some disgruntled customer shouting death and obscenities too horrible to mention after him.

Yes, inevitably there was always someone looking for Foxy with vengeful anger in their faces and no doubt burning inquiries about the quality control of his audio and visual product range.

One day me and Tez spotted Foxy artfully poking his head out of a nearby back alley. "Hey up Foxy!!" me and Tez deliberately enquired at the top of our voices from across the road.
"Keep it down lads!!" whispered Foxy and he artfully beckoned us across the road.
Foxy was still nervously looking up the street. "What up Foxy?" Terry asked in a whisper.
"There's a bloke looking for me," he whispered back.
"Oh, yeah Foxy we've talked to him," I said at him all dramatically.
"Did he like, say anything about me?" Foxy inquired tentatively.
"No, not really," answered Tez with a light voice, and Foxy sighed a little relief, until Tez added quickly, "Just that he was going to smash your face in."
"He asked us where you was?" I said and Foxy's eyes opened wide, "What did you tell him?" he urgently whispered back.
"Nowt," said Tez, "we din't know where you was."
"Did he say owt else to ya like?" asked Foxy gingerly, "Was he angry like?"
"Well yeah, I suppose he was angry," said Tez, "He sort'a mentioned in passing, something about a problem with a telly and ringing your fucking neck."
Me and Tez got the feeling that old man Foxy was looking for some reassurance but all me and Tez saw was an opportunity to make some dosh and I winked at Tez. "He's banging at your door Foxy. Maybe he wants to buy another telly off ya Foxy?" Shall I go fetch him for you?" and I was walking off.
"No! no! no!" Foxy quickly jumped in, and he sort of put on this smarmy smile, like he was trying to pull a fast one on us. "He's bit upset at the moment," said Foxy. "He had a fire in his living room, and he's trying to blame it on one of my products. But I think it's an insurance job."

"Oh, you mean that house down Wellstead street," I went straight back at him, "No Foxy, it wasn't just his living room, half the house went up in smoke."

"Was one of your tellys then Foxy?" said Tez.

"Just a slight technical problem with one of the duffer valves," said Foxy, "I'm working on it with Percy the ragman. Look lads just do us a favour and go tell him I've moved to Manchester."

"But Foxy," Tez spouted up with this angelic face, "that's lying. It's a sin to lie and we're back at Sunday school. We don't want to start off on the wrong foot!"

"Sunday school!!! You two, since when?!!" Foxy retorted.

"Can't tell lies Foxy," I said at him.

"Come lads," said Foxy half pleading, "It's your old mate Foxy asking here?"

"How much is it worth?" Tez suddenly said.

Foxy curled his lip, "I should have known you two wouldn't see the light for long. I'll give ya two bob."

"I tell ya what Foxy," I said taking up my negotiating position, "We'll do it for half a crown."

"Half a crown!" retorted Foxy, and just as he said it, the voice of the man banging on Foxy's door echoed out the terrace, "I'm gonna smash your head in Foxy when I get my hands on you!!" and other disturbing words and profanities of that ilk that gave full narration of the disturbing and imaginative options of violence that are likely to be visited on Foxy's person when this customer of unknown origins gets his hands on him.

And mentally in our little scheming heads, the price was rising with each loud violent outhurst that rang down the street, "Core," said Tez, "he sounds angry."

We are both stood staring at Foxy and he was looking at us with increasing desperation in his face and he dipped his hand into pockets and pulled out a hand full of silver change. Me and Tez's eyes lit up. Foxy picked out a half crown piece and proffered it to Terry. "EACH!" Tez, suddenly piped up.

"EACH!!" Foxy squawked in pain at the thought of being surgically separated from five bob and Foxy stared us out like he wanted to strangle us for taking advantage of his precarious predicament.

And suddenly the sound of breaking glass is coming from Foxy's terrace up the streets. "I think he's smashing ya windows Foxy," I said slowly, "Half a crown each, it's up to you!" And begrudgingly Foxy mumbled and cursed under his breath and handed over another half crown piece. "NOW SOD OFF AND GO TELL HIM I'VE MOVED."

And so having reached and equitable solution on price, me and Tez ran up the street to talk to the bloke banging and now kicking on Foxy's drum.

Now you readers might think we were taking advantage of Foxy in his difficult circumstances but we only had Foxy's interests at heart. When all said and done, Foxy was one of us, a Marmaduke Streeter. We always stuck together and backed each other up. We wouldn't let any harm come to Old Man Foxy. We might have squeezed half a crown each off him but that wasn't much for a grown up and to a little kid on Hessle Road in those days, half a crown was a King's ransom and would mean, goodies, beer and fags for at least two nights and of course we could share our good luck with local lasses in return for an evening's snogging and groping session in Constable Street School.

So when we get round to the terrace and all the neighbours are out, gassing and giving it loads in their household turbans and pinnies in full Hessle Road gassing mode and all standing around with disapproving arms folded and this bloke has smashed Foxy front window and now kicking on his front door as we run up. "Have you two seen him?" this bloke shouts us, "I'm gonna kill him when I get hands on him! I'm gonna knock his teeth so far down his throat he'll need to stick a tooth brush up his arse to clean them."

Me and Tez got the distinct impression this bloke was not happy with electrical equipment as supplied by Messrs Fox & Co distributors of dodgy electric equipment from stock. And this bloke then growls at me and Tez, "If you two know where I can find him, I'll give you half a crown!!"

Tez looked suddenly at me and I suddenly looked at Tez and a big, "Mmmmmm?" instantly went through our greedy little heads. But

Foxy was a mate, a fellow Hessle Road cavalier, one of a band of
brothers, that would be betrayal. And down Hessle Road we all
stuck together, especially when you lived in the same street. Foxy
was one of our own and we would defend him to the last and then
this bloke looks at us and says………, "EACH!"
And me and Terry seemed answer in chorus, "He's hiding down
the alley just up the street."
Sometimes it's just a dog-eat-dog world isn't and you can't trust
anybody. And the next thing, two more half crowns were pushed
into our hungry little mits and this bloke bolted round the corner
with a purpose and the for the next five minutes the screams of a
man in severe distress carried around the street as me and Terry
made our way to the local goody shop, that also sold fags in small
packets of five and also purchased a cheap bottle of plonk and as
planned partied until midnight in the dark doorway entrances of
Constable Street School with two local birds having the lips
snogged of us and as for the rest, you can mind your own
business, but, BOOTS WERE FILLED as the saying goes down our
street.

The next day and Foxy is not spotted until the ambulance pulls up
and Foxy gingerly emerges from the back of the ambulance being
carefully helped by the two ambulance men and into a waiting
wheelchair. Foxy has plasters all over his face, two black eyes and
his arm in a sling.
"What happened Foxy?" we ask all innocent. But Foxy can hardly
talk as his jaw is all wired up and he is hissing angry words
through his wired teeth.
"Fine job you two did!" he snapped sarcastically.
"It wont us Foxy," Tez said back, "We told that bloke you didn't
live there anymore."
"Oh yeah," retorted Foxy, "Well who do you think did this to me,
the fucking tooth fairy." And then Foxy sort of tried to smile as if
he had some consolation for his bodily battering, "Mind you the
bastard din't get his money back," and he mischievously sniggered
to himself and then glared at us. "If I find out you two…" and

before Foxy could finish his threat Tez jumped in. "It wasn't us, cross our hearts and hope to die, but we know who it was."

"Who?!!!" Foxy glared breathing fire.

"Can't say Foxy," I quickly said in curious whisper, 'we're sworn to secrecy." And Foxy goes into his pocket and pulls out a two bob piece and proffers it towards me,

"Here! Here's two bob, now spill the beans!" says Foxy getting all angry and flustered, "I'll kill him."

"Two bob each!" Tez jumps in.

"You two never give up do ya!" and without arguing he goes straight into his pocket again with his one good hand and throws us another two bob piece. "Now give!" Foxy demands emphatically. Me and Tez are looking at each other wondering whose name to give Foxy, and like an offer from the Gods who should walk by but Foxy's life time street enemy Pete Pudding Head, and Pudding Head can't resist a self satisfied snigger at Foxy sitting in the wheel chair looking like a trussed up Egyptian mummy. And me and Tez are thinking the same. We look at Foxy and then nod in Pudding Head's direction, lean towards Foxy and whisper in an accusing, "Who do ya think?"

Foxy grits his teeth and snarls with an angry look of vengeance as he glares at Pudding Head walking past him. "Right!!!" says Foxy with hard purpose, "His fucking card is marked with a big X. Thanks Lads, I knew ya wouldn't let me down." And Foxy is wheeled screeching and squealing as he led away over the lumpy terrace cobble stones.

I suppose we should apologies to readers for being such a duo of two little shit stirrers, but readers have to understand that in two days me and Tez had made seven bob each in hard cash and that was a lot of money in those days for a Hessle Road kid to have in his pocket. And in any case me and Tez both knew that Old Man Foxy couldn't knock a nail in the wall let alone knock Pudding Head out. But Pudding Head did wake up one morning to find his back gate off its hinges and his front parlour window smashed with a big pile of chicken shit dumped in his back yard and the walls of his front parlour pebble dashed with chicken shit and the only geezer that kept chickens down Marmaduke Street was Old Man Foxy.

But thinking back you have to hand it to Old Man Foxy, once you bought a telly off Foxy, you had more chance of getting blood out of stone than getting your money back. It was this lack of a money back guarantee of his dodgy workmanship, that usually accounted for so many scrapes Old Man Foxy got into and would usually end up in Foxy sporting a black eye, fat lip or thick ear, after one of his less than satisfied customers eventually managed to corner him down some dark alley at midnight, and customer feed back usually came into the form of big dirty hairy fist plonking one on his nose and all Marmaduke would know is, that Foxy's blood curdling screams would be heard echoing down the street as Foxy pleaded for mercy as Hessle Road justice sadly caught up with him.

Yes, old Man Foxy too, just like the rest of all us losers down Marmaduke Street, had dreams of big business and hitting the big time and the big money and I think his business model was styled on the Steptoe and Son school of business. And no doubt the telly he thought was a bargain, would end up like all the rest of the useless gear he bought, piled up in his back yard and house collecting dust.

Chapter Five

Now there were lots of people who hated each other down our street. It was the old story and with lots of people at sea and lots of others on the dole or sick, there was always some mucky goings on down our street. Especially after a drinking session in the Criterion and you could guarantee you would spot somebody either dropping her draws for somedody they shouldn't down a local ten foot, or creeping down the street with a neighbour in the darkness for a night of drunken sticky passion. But you couldn't hide much down our street from prying nosey eyes behind the flickering curtains no matter how hard you tried. And sometimes us little kids would walk down the street and the old gossiping gas bags would be out on the doorsteps putting the boot in giving each other the low down who on was jumping in bed with who, whilst hard working hubby was working the over time at some smelly fish house or braving the waves on some deep sea trawler.

But in these present days of female and male liberation, generally both sexes are as bad as each other. In our day, of course, as me and Tez rememeber any lass dropping her draws for a bit of a recreational bonk got known as a slag, and the bloke doing exactly the same dipping his wick got the honour of being known as a stag. But the decent lasses generally kept away from the so-called Hessle Road stags, lest they got a name for themselves. The difference I suppose in our day was both male and female had some sense of shame. They knew what they were doing was wrong, and if you were knocking off some local lass, you could bet if Dad or big brovs found out, you would get the pasting of your life. Today you get a spot on the Jeremy Kyle show and tell millions who has been in your knickers. Oh dear, sorry folks, we slipped into a bit of old fashioned morality there. I suppose what we mean is, illicit bonking has always gone on but in our day it was not something to brag about.

Anyway with all the rumours and gossip going around down our street, it made for some good wind ups, because to many, a bit of gossip was as good as the truth, just so long as the gossip was malicious it mattered not if it was the truth or not. Just so long as it was juicy, hot and generally had something do with sex or some such mucky going on. But with our gang it was the street characters we were always winding up and playing off against each other for nothing more than a laugh. And this rumour about Pete Pudding head and his mother's body being kept in an upstairs bed room was running rampant down Marmaduke Street, and it was just too tempting to wind up Old Man Foxy with latest off the gossip news wires. Foxy was just so gullible to anything you might tell him. Just wind him up and pointing him the right direction and of course after the legendary Foxy/Pudding Head debacle over the telly that Foxy had sold and blow up and burnt half that blokes house down, and Foxy thinking that it was Pudding Head who had dobbed him in it as to his whereabouts, meant you could tell Foxy almost anything about Pudding Head and he would swallow it. And what better to wind up Old Man Foxy about was, that his next door neighbour Pudding Head could be a night stalking, cross-dressing knife toting nutter.

And what do you know, but who is this ambling down the street pushing his pram, but that high flying deal breaker of the local sale rooms and rag yards, but Old Man Foxy after another successful international business trip selling broiler chickens to the Arabs and cornering the London market on busted televisions in the cut and thrust of Hessle Road's cosmopolitan and cultural quarter of Coltman Street.

So as Foxy is moseying and whistling along and at piece and contentment with the world and minding his own business and so me and Tez pelt down Marmaduke Street to catch up with him and we're out of breath when we catch up with him.

"Now then you two," says Foxy all startled, "Where's the fire!" Terry is all out of breath, "Hey Foxy, have you seen Pudding Head?"

You only have to mention Pudding Head's name and people down Marmaduke Street people would freeze. Old Man Foxy's eyes open wide with fear. "No, and I fucking don't want to either. It's bad enough the Twat living next door to me. His fucking house stinks!" Now that's the kettle calling the pot black by anyone's standards as Foxy wasn't exactly known for his own personal hygiene or being a house-proud fairy either. And now we had Foxy on the hook and his eyes go all wide and curious, "That Pudding Head is a bit weird if you ask me," Foxy whispers at us all dramatic. "Not all there upstairs if you get my meaning. Have you heard what he gets up to with that dog at night? It's disgusting, he wants reporting to the RSPCA."

"Never mind that," says Tez all dark and curious, and his voice goes straight into full wind up mode and it takes on a sinister low tone, as Terry starts his little horror story. "Have you heard the latest?"

And Foxy is suddenly all ears and eyes wide open and bulging in expectant horror. "No, what?" he said leaning forward and biting hard.

"Sweaty Betty reckons Pudding Head's mother has been dead for years," says Tez, "and is stuck up in the front bedroom."

"Fucking 'ell," retorts Foxy with a big in take of breath. "That could be the bleedin' stink then," Foxy snapped back in horror, "but she can't be dead, I hear 'em talking through the walls on a night."

Terry leans into Foxy's face, "Are you sure Foxy?" he whispers in an eerie voice.

"Er what do ya mean?" Foxy whispers back harshly.

"Well you fink about this," says Tez all sinister, "it could be Pudding Head taking her off, couldn't it?" whispers Tez all sinister and dramatic.

And Foxy is stood there with his eyes throbbing and bulging out their sockets and scared shitless, holding onto his pram so tightly and shaking so much that the second hand television tied to his pram almost fell off. And he says all trembly, "It's just like Him in that movie in't it, that Psycho movie," said Foxy all twitchy.

"You mean Norman Bates!" Terry suddenly blurts out in harsh whisper.

"Yeah, that's him," says Foxy all trance-like, "Norman Bates."

"You wanna be careful Foxy," said Tez imitating an eerie voice. "Make sure you lock ya doors Foxy," and Tez starts up all slow, "you could be in ya bed, and out of the black a cold sweaty hand comes over you in the darkness, and you, thinking it's your lass after you feeding the hedge hog, and instead of a quick poke, you feel the cold slash of steel swishing at your flesh and the next he's tickling your bones with a one foot carving knife, everything goes black and you wake up bollock naked tied to the dining table in Pudding Head's front parlour, all trussed up with Pudding Head using your ribs for a xylophone. And in the blackness…You see…It's…it's… PUDING HEAD!!! Dressed up as his mother!!" "FUCKING 'ELL!!!" Foxy gawps back all wide eyed and staring. And with that he quickly slopes off, but then stops for a second and turns back round to us, "Hey, you two," and winks and whispers, "Ya don't know anyone who wants a telly do you?" We both slowly shake our heads, and then come his next stock question, "You ain't got a fag to spare have ya?" Again we both shake our heads and Foxy minces off and he is a man now a man on a mission to secure his family and more importantly, protect his priceless artifacts from harm and looting from the nutter next door.

And all that afternoon until dark all you could hear from Foxy's house was loud banging and clattering back way and front way as Foxy feverishly slammed up more bolts on the doors than Fort Knox, and around 7 o'clock he emerged in the terrace all hot and sweaty in his mucky grey string vest and gives us a dopey thumbs up with a big self satisfied smile and proffers at us this big fuck off base bat and starts swinging it about with all the bravado of a Ninja assassin. "Just let the bastard Pudding Head try now, he'll get his head examined with this." And then retreats back to his hovel with the usual nut case smile on his face, closed his front door and all you could hear was slam, slam, slam, slam, slam, slam, click, rattle and roll and Fox's front door was certainly locked and hopefully Pudding Head proof. And me and Tez walked away laughing in stitches.

Whilst me and Tez have to admit that all that the rumours and gossip that followed Pudding Head around could have been just malicious shit stirring by the locals as gossip, gassing, name calling was a past time and me and Tez have to admit that back stabbing was just par for the course down Marmaduke Street. But one thing was known for sure about Pete Pudding Head. And that was he had been caught "midging" outside of Boyes store just around the corner of Marmaduke Street and after a scuffle and some loud denials he had been carted off kicking and screaming in a "meat wagon" by the coppers to Gordon street cop shop and whilst he was not charged with the "midging" he was sporting a black eye and a fat lip for a week or so, because if there was one thing coppers in those days hated it was "midging" and was regarded as a serious sexual perversion.

For all Pudding Head's faults and all the unfounded rumours about him, as a perv, a midger and sex maniac, he had all the qualities that today would have qualified him as one hell of a politician. Today Pudding Head for all his short comings would have probably been the Labour MP for west Hull and likely made a spiffing job for his constituents. Instead now we have that other bloke, what's his name now, oh yes, Allan Johnson but let's not get too depressed about that, it could be John Prescott, so old Allan Jonno might not be so bad after all. And Jonno is nice bloke but me and Tez know he doesn't like us because we sell more books than him.

Well, whether or not Pudding Head would be considered in today's sexually liberated climate, a pervert or trend setter, we will leave up to history to decide and that is only right and just, as one man's meat is another man's poison. And on Hessle Road in those days and we had more than our fair share of perverts in all shapes and sizes and sexes.

I suppose there will be many out there that are not familiar with the old Hessle Road term of "midging". Now I have to stress here that whilst we and many others from those long gone halcyon days of the early 1960s will be familiar with the term "Midging", me and Tez stress that it was never a pass time either we or our mates dabbled in, and we say that most sincerely folks and you will understand why in a moment.

So what is "midging" me and Tez hear many of you readers cry inquisitively? Well now that might be a difficult one for us to describe and for all those out there with a delicate disposition, the practice might be just too psychologically distressing to read. So we will tread carefully in our run up to narrating what a midger is. And for those readers who can take no more as they read, they can skip to the next pages, where there is a telephone number of a BBC help line for those who have been emotionally distressed or disturbed, as they have help lines for everything else these days.

Though we can't give you the legal or psychological term for this dastardly practice of midging, what we can divulge to you, is that it does involve ladies riding bicycles. And me and Tez stress here ladies riding bicycles and not men, no definitely not men. So let's us look in more detail and take a scientifically forensic analytical view at the modus operandi of a "midger" and you may well get a better idea of what a MIDGER is. We don't want to shroud our description in prejudice or be judgmental, this is 2016 after all and anything goes. After all there are many sexual oddities accepted today that were considered a sexual perversion in the 1960s and are now in these more enlightened accepted as near normal today. I mean look at Westminster or the House of Lords, but let's not get too distracted and return to the matter in hand because we could all spend all day slagging that lot off.

Now just before we start our narration of what a "midger" is, we would wish to give notice to those readers of a delicate disposition. So with this in mind, this is what we intend to do. Do you remember when you went to the cinema in the 1960s with a bird to see a horror film and as the screams and blood would be sloshing around the screen, and suddenly the film would stop, and a great booming dramatic voice would echo from the movie, "WE WARN VIEWERS THAT THE SCENES THAT FOLLOW MAY BE OF A DISTURBING NATURE AND IF YOU ARE OF A NERVOUS DISPOSITION, YOU HAVE THIRTY SECONDS TO LEAVE THE CINEMA."

And a ticking clock would come on the cinema screen counting down the thirty seconds to give you time to bolt for the exit. But you would all sit there scared shitless, with you eyes bulging in horror and with your girlfriend holding onto you for grim death watching the ticking clock count down the seconds. Well that is what we are going to do now.

WILL ALL READERS OF A NERVOUS DISPOSITION PUT DOWN THIS BOOK OR SKIP TO THE NEXT CHAPTER."

(NOW YOU HAVE TO PRETEND A CLOCK IS TICKING NOW.)

"TICK, TICK, TICK, TICK…TIMES UP READERS!!"

So here we go then and we once again warn those of a sensitive and nervous disposition to think carefully before reading on. YOU HAVE BEEN WARNED and you read on at your own risk.

A "midger" is generally not a happy creature and is somewhat of a tortured spirit with deeply and fiercely repressed sexual urgings of an unnatural nature. And often they become nocturnal creatures and may stalk the night looking to vent the animal urgings throbbing in their pants. So consumed with their obsessive search for ladies bicycles they will often self neglect, become smelly, rarely change their under pants and reject the world that is so unforgiving of their horrible practices, and so they will often be a loner. No surprise there then. They tend to work on their sinister practice in isolation, and only rarely have they been known to hunt in packs and will chose their target carefully. And they might well have stalked their female prey for days with an amorous evil look of nefarious intent on their minds. And homed in, they will choose their moment to strike carefully, and usually when the female on the bicycle has dismounted and climbed off said bicycle, and leaned it innocently against a wall or outside a shop, the "midger" will wait for the victim to leave the bicycle and then in an uncontrollable frenzy rush up to said bicycle and take a great big hearty sniff of the seat, and that is "midging" in a nutshell.

More serious serial "midgers" have been known to go tooled up and carrying adjustable spanners so they can not only have a good sniff of the seat, but purloin the bike seat and slink off quickly home on tip toe with the bike seat tucked under their long black overcoat as they melt like a ghoulish phantom into the crowds of happy shoppers oblivious to the felonious deed perpetrated under their noses. Like many serial sex fiends, the bike seat may be considered as taken as a sort of trophy so they can "midge" to their hearts content in the comfort of their own home, perhaps whilst taking in the pleasures of watching Hughie Green's Opportunity Knocks, or Sunday Night At The London Palladium with Brucie Forsyth. And why not, some people smoke or puff on pipe whilst watching the box and what's wrong with that. It is no more than you deserve after a hard day's work at the Hessle Road Road coal face as it were. And the Midger too needs his R & R too, just because you are a raving sex pervert does not mean you are not entitled to enjoy the fruits of your perversion and the more simplistic Midgers will simply sit there in a darkened room heartily sniffing a bike seat, usually though not exclusively, stark bollock naked in front of a blazing fire having a good old tug on his plonker, as you do when all is well with the world.

But excess is usually the down fall of many midgers and me and Tez are of the opinion, that Pudding Head was, after years of getting away with it, had become so emboldened by years of getting away with it, that he became just too clever for his own good. And the problem was that he was just going over the top and nicking so many bicycle seats that a moral panic was breaking out down Hessle Road that a serial midger was on the loose, and then there was the uncomfortable ride home for the ladies and painful too if they forgot the seat was missing on peddle back to base to explain why the old man's eggs and chips were late on the table.

After exhaustive enquiries by the local flat foots at Gordon Street Cop Shop, and acting on a mysterious tip off, they got a sniff of their own and crashed through Pudding heads door on a midnight raid and caught Pudding Head red handed feverishly sniffing on the female fumes exuding from a newly purloined bicycle seat with a sinister relish like an opium addict who had not had a fix for days, and the case was cracked.

Yes, the day they caught Pudding was a real red letter for the local plods and as baying crowds gathered at the top of the terrace down Marmaduke Street and Pudding Head was led away in handcuffs, his head covered with a blanket to a waiting cop car to a flashing battery of cameras of the nations media and of course the good old local and trusty news hounds of the Hull Daily Mail. A sigh of relief could be heard down Hessle Road as the cloud of dark fear and trepidation that had pitted neighbour against neighbour in climate of fear and suspicion that had stalked the old road for years lifted across Hessle Road. And once again, in England's green and pleasant land, the upstanding fish factory lasses and buxom maidens of Hessle Road were once again free to ride their cycles without having their personages molested by Peter Pudding Head.
Yes, many on that memorable day in 1967 breathed a big sigh of relief and was so aptly summed in the immortal words of that other Hessle Road legend, Whispering Jack The Flash, as he turned to his mate known famously as Radish standing next to him, "Thank fuck they got him Radish," said Jack shaking his head, "I would have sworn it was you." And full descriptions of both Messer's Radish and Whispering Jack will be coming soon and are not to be missed.

As you can imagine Pudding Head twisted and turned under pressured questioning and claimed he only sniffed the bicycle seats purely for medicinal purpose, as a good deep sniff cleared his snotty and bogie blocked up sinuses. When questioned further and asked why he didn't just use Vic like everybody else, Pudding Head claimed he didn't know Vic had a bike. But our local plods were tenacious and nobody's fools, and Pudding Head just had no reasonable answer for the aforementioned argument. And taboot, also this did not explain why he had his pants and skiddies around his ankles feverishly "creaming one off" in mid-sniff when the plods had crashed through his front door. Yes, the evidence was stacking up against Pudding Head as well as the bike seats. Now what happened next would take some explaining even for Pudding Head, and rumour had it that on the advice of his brief, Pudding Head took the "fifth" and stayed stumb and according to the local gossips down Marmaduke street, especially Sweaty Betty, she claimed the plods recovered over twenty bike seats from the walls of Pudding Head's living room, where it would seem he had mounted them on the wall much like a Great White Hunter would mount animal heads. And to everyone's surprise, they even recovered Sweaty Betty's bicycle seat but not mounted on the wall but welded to a washing mangle in Pudding Head's bedroom. So Pudding Head at least had some taste and it seemed Sweaty Beatty's anal aromas were definitely to his liking or sniffing tastes, and maybe he was still holding a torch for his teenage lost love, Sweaty Betty. But me and Terry have a little sympathy for Pudding Head on that one because it did not excuse the reign of terror his Midging had wrought across Hessle Road. But at least this shameful episode was over, for now anyway and the good ladies of Hessle Road took once again to riding their bicycles free from the threat of being midged by Pudding Head.

Now me and Tez hear shouts of the skeptical crying outrage and disbelief from the reader's gallery, that such a practice as "midging" (also known as "SNURGING") exists, "I don't believe it!" we hear readers out there cry. "These lying bastards Ian Newton and Terry Cox are just making it up." Well don't be so hasty with shouting your slanderous cries of, "Liars!!" and look at this our old mates and we expect an apology for the aspersions cast on our characters by the disbelievers out there. So here, stick this in your pipe and smoke it. Me and Tez have Googled it for you and so you can check it for yourself here. With the two Internet hits we have cut and pasted them for your comfortable perusal and purely academic interest. And like us, you will no doubt come to the conclusion at what a real pickle the world has got itself into when some innocent young women cannot ride her bike to the shops in England's hollowed streets without being accosted by a MIDGER. And no doubt there will be those lady cyclists who will now take heed and more care that they are not being watched with more than passing interest as they park their bicycles and go in search of the sausages and mash for their hard working hubby's tea. Now ladies we issue here a word of caution, either read on, or for those females of a more delicate disposition please turn to the next page now if you are easily offended. But for those ladies made of sterner stuff please feel free to read onward. So ladies, next time parking up your bike beware of the "MIDGER" and take heed, he could be watching you. Now read below.

Google search: (Midger or Snurgler)

1.   Urban Dictionary: **saddle sniffer**www.urbandictionary.com/define.php?term=**saddle +sniffer   +midger** A person (most likely a man) who gets sexual gratification from **sniffing bicycle saddles**. They **sniff** the material and imagine a woman sitting on it only moments earlier...

Bike Porn [Archive] - Mountain **Bike** Rider Forumswww.mbr.co.uk/forums/archive/index.php/t-7007.html?s... **Midge**. 01-Dec-2010, 05:11 PM. Cycle Passion (http://www.cyclepassion.com/): roll eyes: ... OMG there is an actual word for **sniffing bike seats**!

So not only was old Pete a consummate Pudding Head but a man who took his Midging seriously, but if you ever wanted a cheap bicycle seat it was always worth a knock on Pudding Heads door as he could usually do you a bargain. Let us now go forth and move on in search of more tall tales of Hessle Road and the long gone ghosts of time that once walked there before those bloody Turkish Barbers moved in.

Chapter Six

Now, as promised in earlier pages and as read about in earlier editions of the Hessle Road Scallywags, it is not possible to write about Hessle Road's Marmaduke Street, without mentioning the following two memorable characters that walked in the historical smoky fog of Hessle Road and Marmaduke Street of the 1960's.

Yes, there is no point denying it, Radish was a bit of a sad character and I am sure many readers will remember him from the first Hessle Road Scallywags book. He was totally harmless to man or beast and no joking, he looked like one of those pin men you used to draw in infant school and although he liked to pretend he was a hard case, it just didn't work when he came on all hard case like when you gave him some cheeky lip to wind him up and then reel him in.

One day me and Terry spotted him coming down the street with his long time mate and other general sad bastard Whispering Jack. Forty odd year old Whispering Jack is well a passed his sell by date as a Teddy boy that has never grown up, and is like frozen in time. Poor old Whispering Jack just cannot accept that his Teddy Boy time is long gone, and like some lost traveler in time, still has all the Teddy Boy gear on and his hair greased back like a poor man's Billy Fury and they both are on their regular nightly lass-pulling-patrol down Marmaduke Street. It was a sad sight indeed to watch as they sauntered along our street like a couple of weirdo toss pots, living in the forlorn hope that some unlikely female would be so overcome with their charms and irresistible animal charisma, that they would allow them to empty their bulging sacks in a nearby alley.

Yes, you have to admire these two tryers, they just never gave up with the ugly duckies down our street and would deploy quiet few inducements to curry favour with the local "bikes", of which there were many in those days. And they would walk down the street with a self-deluding posers swagger chewing on bubble gum and puffing on a half smoked Woodbine to look cool and smiling at the lasses, like they were God's gift. And I must say their chat up lines were hardly original, "Do you want to come and see some puppies," never quite clicked with the local lasses with two pairs of glaring eyes and a duo of sharp black and yellow nashers staring back at you. I suppose they didn't have much left in the chat up armory after they got rid of the ice cream van after the local coppers had cleared them off from outside the local girls' school.

But indeed some of the local totty did certainly succumb to a free night in the Criterion Pub getting pissed on the free drinks being poured down their neck by the lusting Radish and a knob-throbbing Whispering Jack. But alas it would be an endless fools errand by the two pub court jesters, and come the bell for "time on ya beer" the lasses would bolt faster than Speedy Gonzalez being chased by the hapless Loony Tunes cartoon cat Sylvester, and the only thing they no doubt ending up shagging was their right hand after retiring lucklessly to bed with the only variation in the bedtime routine of self sexual gratification, being if they used their left hand instead of the right hand, since it usually felt like someone else was tugging you off.

So now that we have described them, how could we as kids resist taking the piss and winding them up. It was just not possible.
"Hey up Radish," said Tez in a piss taking voice.
Now Radish doesn't like being called by his nickname of Radish, especially by a little kid and instantly goes into hard case mode. And snaps back in his, deep back of throat gravelly, dopey voice "Hey you, ya cheeky little bastard who are you calling Radish!!"
"That's ya fucking name in't it Radish," I pipe up.
"No it fucking isn't," and he comes right up to us, but we're not scared but his diarrhea bad breath sprays into our faces like a fire dragon and we lurched backwards to avoid the fumes. "Nobody calls me Radish and gets away with it." And just as he says that a local hard knock walks by and greets him with. "Now then Radish!" and instantly Radish smiles back, "Alright mate."
"Well he's just called you Radish," says Tez.

"He's me mate," says Radish all abashed, "And you're not, that's the difference."

"He's not your mate Radish," I smarmed back at him, "you're just scared of him."

"I'll knock your fucking block off in a minute," Radish threatens us. "It's a good job Jack's holding me back, or I'd paste ya!"

Old dopey Whispering Jack is stood there like a ten-gallon tosser puffing on a woodbine, "Just a minute Radish, I'm not holding you back."

"No, he's not holding you back Radish," repeats Tez, putting up his fists,

"I tell ya this," says, Radish in an over dramatic voice, "when I start, I just go mad and I know Jack will just jump in and stop me, 'cause he knows I'm an animal when I start, I don't know when to stop."

So we both put up our dooks and start bouncing around Radish throwing shadow punches at him. "Come on then Radish put 'em up, there's two us, see if ya can take us on."

Radish looks at Whispering Jack, "Well there's two of us as well."

"Now leave me outa this Radish," says Whispering Jack stepping back. "Not with my bad back, I'm on painkillers now you know, and I've got a sick note."

"Come on then," we both shout at Radish, "put 'em up or shut up!"

"Ya don't want to get me mad," says Radish, "Last time a bloke did that, all I saw was this foggy black mist and after the mist cleared someone was laid in pool of blood flat out on the floor."

"Who was it Radish," shouts Tez, "YOU!!"

"If I didn't have me best suite on," says Radish backing off, "I'd give you two a good hiding. Just don't call me Radish and I won't belt you."

"You touch us Radish," Terry snarls back, "and our kid will do you both."

"Just a minute," Whispering Jack croaks up, "It's Radish causing the trouble not me."

"I ain't causing trouble," says Radish and Tez jumps in, "Jack's just called you Radish!"

Radish turns on Whispering Jack all hard and threatening, "Did you just call me Radish?"

"But I'm your mate Radish," Jack answers and Radish turns back to me and Tez, "Yeah, that's right, Jack's me mate."

Then Whispering Jack pipes up, "Radish doesn't like being called Radish, especially by little kids. So just say sorry and we won't smack you up."

Tez goes right up to Whispering Jack's face and take his fag out of his mouth, and sucks in a drag then blows it right into Jack's face. "You touch us and my big brother will kill ya!" Now Terry's big brother is one big hard bastard with muscles like Popeye after eating spinach.

"Now," says Whispering Jack, all suddenly nervous smiles, "Now come on lads, there's no need for that. Just don't call Radish, Radish, he don't like it."

"No, that right," says Radish, "I don't like being called Radish."

"Alright then," says Tez, "We won't call you Radish then Radish. Is that a fair deal Radish?

"And I won't call you Radish either Radish," I pipe up.

"So that's a deal then?" and Radish holds out his hand for a shake. Me and Tez look at each. "It's deal Radish, we promise not to call you Radish again Radish!" And we walk off, "See ya Radish." Radish smiles like he has won, "See ya kids."

And without further a do, Radish and Whispering Jack waddle off down the street in the self deluding swagger of two daft blokes who think they look irresistible to the local female totty as they saunter along for a night's patrol down our street, with their fanny radar switched on looking for any available bird under ten feet tall who was hard up enough to drop their knickers for them, and there was little hope of that.

You would think the way Radish used to dress he was going for a night on the town to a posh club as he would wear this smart silver suite with tight thin drainpipe trousers and a shirt and tie. The tie I always thought was a bit over the top for a night on the prowl down Marmaduke Street and the only people I had seen wearing ties down Marmaduke was Stuttering Joe on his way to court or the bailiffs lifting his telly for either non payment of the rental or treating the TV coin box as a piggy bank.

Radish lived and died in that suite and anyone else would have looked the dog's bollocks wearing it but with Radish being so tall and skinny he just looked like a pipe cleaner. He had these massive ears and a real gargoyle face and was also so ugly that he would have made the Hunchback of Notre Dame look like Carry Grant and he had this really strange way of talking from the back of his throat with a real deep gravel voice that always sounded so serious. He and Whispering Jack liked to hang out with Bazza and Minnie because they always held on to the hope that they could get one of their female cast-offs and some sloppy seconds and they were always perving around the girls in the street with a sweety bag full of Pineapple chunks or mint imperials as if the lasses down our street would come so cheap.

Now it was Terry who reminded of this story and I had totally forgotten about it. Radish did not have many mates that were not fair weather, especially when Radish had been paid on a Friday and had some greens and blues in his arse hole pocket. Oh yes on payday Radish could count his friends on all his ten nicotine brown fingers. Now we are not saying the girls down our street were especially mercenary when it came to a man with money, but we have to admit that the Marmaduke Street lasses especially would come on a lot friendlier to Radish as pay day closed in. Yes, they could be a little bit tricky Marmaduke Street lasses, and they would woo Radish with flirtatious smiles, short skirts and big, thick, silky riding thighs in black boots, as an indication of sexual possibilities if Radish paid for the drinks all night in Criterion on a Friday night out.

And no matter how many times the tarts down our street took Radish and Whispering Jack for a ride on a night of free drinks, the hapless duo always fell for the same old trick. I suppose with the pulsating pork truncheon throbbing away in their trousers they lived in hope of dipping their wick into something, anything. But of course the luckless pair as always shit out big and sloppy time, and if they thought they was on a promise for "banging the beaver", after paying for the night of frivolity and booze flowing like water, there was always another angle coming with Hessle Road lasses.

And the routine would go something like this. Radish and Whispering Jack would whizz off to the bogs for a quick slash, and the enthusiastic and ever hopeful purchase of pack of three rubber Johnies as they sniggered and giggled away at each other in the bogs, only to realize, after previously rejoining the birds with an easy wink and a confident, "Back in a minute babes." And off they would saunter back into the saloon, only to return to find their fair maidens of Marmaduke Street had disappeared like a fart in the breeze on a windy River Humber jetty.

But it was not just the lasses who took Radish for a ride but Radish's bosom feckless friend Jack, or as us kids called him, "Whispering Jack Flash" because as soon as it was his turn to buy a round Jack suddenly got a weak bladder, and he was gone in a flash too.

Now as I have previously said we called him Whispering Jack for a very good reason, because he always talked like he had a sore throat, much like Don Corleone in The God Father, but of course not as scary. Like Radish in many respects, Whispering Jack was a bit of a lonesome sad bastard and I suppose Radish and Whispering Jack complimented each other much like those on screen losers Laurel and Hardy. Like Laurel and Hardy, Radish and Whispering Jack never knew when the game was up with the lasses, and neither of them were ever, ever going to get their leg over with anything down Marmaduke Street except maybe Pudding Head's dog, and we think Pudding Head would have had something to say about that, if not the dog.

Whispering Jack being a bit of an out-of-date Teddy Boy from the 1950's was living on mental past glories of his sexual exploits when he would ride about Hessle Road as a tear away teenager on his Harley Davidson 500 just like in the film, The Wild One with Marlon Brando and there was even a rumour that Whispering Jack had been an extra in the film. And yes, you've guessed Old

Whispering Jack would have given Billy Liar a run for his money with his delusions and it cut little ice with the local birds in any case. And the truth be known, the closest Whispering Jack had ever got to owning a Harley Davidson, was his old style first world war sit up and beg push bike with a metal basket on the front that he was regularly seen riding, "whilst his motorbike was being repaired" In fact when you asked Whispering Jack where his motor bike was, it was always being repaired. Although to give Jack some credit, he had been known to walk about Hessle Road in his motorbike leathers carrying a crash helmet and swinging a set of keys on his fingers and the only thing missing from the picture was a motorbike of any description.

Radish and Whispering Jack just never learned their lesson with the lasses down our street and I suppose that's what sexual desperation does to you. The pair of them just could not help falling for the same line week after week, and with same results; a long walk home in the cold of a Hessle Road dark Winter's night, with the Humber wind whistling up your jacksey, and with one hell of a big hard on throbbing in your pants at the thought of yet another missed opportunity of getting your end away. And the only thing warm, wet and sloppy they would be getting stuck into would be a cup of Rosy Lea and a Ginger nut biscuit. And so, off they would slope into the night, backs hunched in yet another defeat, mumbling and grumbling and blaming each for another missed opportunity with lases of our street.
And so would endeth another Friday night in the usual routine, and so it would be off to bed for the intrepid dynamic duo, with only the company of their right hands and their imagination to look forward to as, they would retire alone to their pits and feverishly pull the head off it in their lonely beds with the nearest thing for female company being the young hot little girlies on knickers pages of a their old Mum's Littlewoods catalogue splayed open across the blankets and a box of tissues on stand by. And so they tugged away by the light of a candle flickering on the bedside table, because you could put bets on it, they had come home with

empty pockets and not so much as a bob to put into the electric meter.

Now this is interesting, the really funny thing was what Whispering Jack didn't know was, that as he laid on top of his midnight pit pulling the life out his pulsing plonker, the candle next to his bed would project a great big giant black shadow onto his curtains and all the neighbours and us kids would gather across the road watching this big black shadow on Jack's curtains creaming one off with a vengeance. There were more neighbours in the street watching what was going on in Whispering Jack's bedroom via the shadow on his curtains than were watching the midnight movie. And so as the drunks rolled down Constable Street they would accumulate with the rest of us looking up at Jack's window in fascination.

"He's always tearing the head off it, is Jack," said one drunk looking up, "I bet his bell end looks like the Rocky Mountains. Just look at it, it's the size of a fireman's helmet."

And the next morning Jack would emerge out of his front door in his blue work overalls ready for another Monday to Friday at the fish house squelching fish heads and pushing his old trusty bike into in the street for his peddle to work and whistling away all innocent, and bid a big hearty "Morning luv," to all the street fish wives going to work that passed his door, only to be met with the disapproving disgusted stares and cries of, "Ya dirty bastard!" And then another disgusted fishwife would give him short shrift, "You want to see a doctor you do. You'll be going blind. Why you want locking up!"

And Whispering Jack would just stand there all mystified, "What the fuck did I do?!!!"

Poor old Whispering Jack, he just never had the luck with the ladies and now the entire street knew what he got up to, in what should be the private sanctuary of his own bedroom.

As previously stated Whispering Jack was about 40 odd years old and still lived with his mother in a decrepit two-up-two-down in the street next to Marmaduke Street, Constable Street. Whilst greatly looking a lot older than his 40 years, he acted about 20 years old and dressed the part with his partly bald quiffed up hair combed back into a duck's arse style and a long draped Teddy boy jacket, with thick crepe-soled brothel creeping shoes. Yes, poor old Jack loved himself and would saunter down the street in his Teddy boy gear with Radish riding shot gun in his immaculate silver grey suite and tie, and they both must have felt like the bee's knees, and the two doe balls actually thought all the girls were looking at them. And they were, but not for the reasons they thought. The girls and everybody really just thought they looked like a right pair 24 karat gold plated toss pots, well up for being endlessly fleeced of a few lager and limes down the Criterion. But enough for the moment of Whispering Jack the Flash and Radish, let's make some introductions of characters down our long gone street.

Now as mentioned in the first book, Hessle Road Scallywags, Stuttering Joe was always good for us kids to wind up because he was a was a real miserable old bastard and always moving us kids on if we were playing football outside his house. And would emerge on the doorstep, full of hell, "You fffffffffffucking kids gggggggo and ppplay outside your own house. I don't want you putting my windows in. Now fuck off or you'll feel the back of my hand." But sometimes Stuttering Joe was too loose with his mouth for his own good and after shifting us on one night had called me a nigger and said something to one of the lads about his mother. Well after that Stuttering Joe never had any reason to worry about his windows being broken, because me and my mate sneaked out in the early hours and put bricks through all of his windows and he seemed to do a little less complaining until the council fixed his windows some weeks later and he was back at again and shifting us from playing football outside his house.

Across the street from Stuttering Joe was old Jimmy. God only knows how old Jimmy was. He looked over a hundred but was little, lean and mean and bounced around on the balls of his feet wearing these ob-nail boots like a featherweight boxer. If anybody remembers Billy Whiz the comic strip character, he looked just like him and could move just as fast when you knocked on his door and ran away. He would be opening his front door before you had finished knocking and would chase you down the street at full pelt mumbling incoherently and frothing at the mouth and if he caught you he would knock ten bells of shit out of you. And if your Dad or big brother came round complaining he would give them a good kicking too. It was like an initiation ceremony for new kids to the street to get them play "Knock off Ginger" on Jimmy's door and run. "Go on we'd say, he's only an old man." They'd knock and zoom Jimmy would be out the door like a whippet after a hare. There were few he did not catch and that was what made it so much fun and I think maybe in his own way Jimmy enjoyed it too, especially pasting us kids when he caught us.

Now here's a funny story about old Radish, Whispering Jack and the forever complaining Stuttering Joe that might tickle you. It was not unusual for us kids to be out in the street till all hours piss balling about and generally making everybody's life a misery. It was just par for the course in those days as there was fuck all else to do. Now one late night and us kids are out late and playing cricket using a tennis ball under the streetlights just outside Stuttering Joe's house using the street light base as the wicket. Stuttering Joe has been out twice in his mucky string vest shouting the odds and trying to move us on but retreated under the barrage of abuse. Stuttering Joe does a lot of shouting and screaming at us kids when he can get his words out but he's a total paper tiger and us kids know it. But you have to watch out now and again because after old Joe has had a couple of bottles of his home brew fire water that could take paint off door quicker than a blow lamp, he could get filled with so much Dutch courage he thought he was a Hull Fair bare knuckle fighter and would come out baring his fists and start drunkenly bobbing and weaving in the middle of road shadow boxing himself, "Come on then son, you just try putting one on me chin, you just try," and he'd wave his fist at you, "And you'll get this right in the snozzler." And a loud mocking cheer would go up from the kids outside his house, "Ohhhhhhhh!" and all the kids would get round him a circle and shadow box him as Stuttering Joe retreated back to his front door, "I'm telling ya, I'm telling ya now, I used to be Yorkshire boxing champion."

Old Stuttering Joe thinks because he has got POLICE CAUTION notice in his window it will scare us kids. In those days a POLICE CAUTION NOTICE in your window was supposed to put the frighteners on nuisance kids, local thieves and burglars to make it look like the coppers were watching. But the stupid thing was most of the thieves and burglars lived down our street anyway. I suppose a POLICE CAUTION notice in someone's front window in those days was a bit like those signs today that say, "WE ARE A COMMUNITY WATCH NEIGHBOURHOOD" and like it really scares the burglars? And the POLICE CAUTION in Stuttering Joe's window never stopped a few bricks going through his window in the dark hours if his abuse got too personal.

So anyway, this night is no different to any other night down Marmaduke Street really and us scruffy little kids are all shouting and screaming and the local lasses are there too playing hopscotch with some showing their little girly blue school knickers as they do hand stands against the wall and that was always worth watching. As usual the street tribe of local inbred grown-ups are out in force on their doorsteps shouting and swearing at us to watch their mucky windows with ball and with cries of, "And why don't you go and play outside your own house." And, "Smash my windows and you'll be paying for 'em, ya little bastards'!" and all such warnings are met with the usual Hessle Road response

"Oh fuck off in Missis ya fat bastard!! It's only a tennis ball," someone shouts and no one takes any notice, since most of those complaining have hardly any windows left anyway. "I don't care if it is a tennis ball, if you smash my windows and my Bert will be round your house.!!!, And they'll be trouble I'm telling you, ya' cheeky little bastards. I know where you live."

"Eh Missis," one of the gang shouts from the dark, "I've just seen your old man shagging Sweaty Betty down the fish shop alley!"

"What My Bert?" she shouts back. "Well we'll see about that!!" And the fat old bag is off down the road walking with purpose towards Fish Shop alley rolling up her sleeves and clenching her fist. And we tell no lies, Bert is down the back alley with Sweaty Betty bouncing her fat arse off the wall with her knickers and his pants around their ankles going at it hammer and tongs.

So meanwhile back at the cricket match outside Stuttering Joe's house and Tez is bowling and I'm slogging the ball all over the place with kids running around fielding and I'm making a million runs. And I'm also showing off a bit cause my on/off bird Polo is watching me. Now me and Polo are not an item or anything and between you and me she ain't much to look at either, but she has one hell of a nymph little body and she knows just how to use it when you are in a dark doorway having a snog on a night. And she will get all amorous and start pressing her self all over you and at 12 years old, it sort of gets you going if you know what I mean. Now I don't were Polo gets the idea from, but she thinks me and her are serious and she is still always pestering me to come baby sitting with her. And as I said before she has this way of getting round me when I turn her down, and she will just stand there and lift up her skirt so you get a full view of her knickers, and she will smile and say with a dirty grin, "Just think what you'll be missing Ian." So with an offering like that I spent many a night baby sitting in various houses around our street sprawled out on couch snogging the gob off Polo, as we dry humped each other with our clothes on not too sure what we were doing but thoroughly enjoying it anyway. And was she one hell of a snogger, but because she wasn't much in the looks department I always insisted on snogging with the lights off and pretending she was one of the birds out the Pans People dancers on Top of the Pops. I don't know who was your favourite in Pan's People but mine was always hot blonde one they called Babs. But have to admit I wouldn't have thrown any of them out of my bed, not that I had many girls in my bed at twelve years old, but certainly had plenty in my head as you tend to at that age.

Anyway, enough of Polo for the moment and let's go back to the cricket match and I'm still slogging Terry's bowling all over the shop. And then who should come moseying down the street but the dastardly duo of Radish and Whispering Jack. Both of them can't take their eager little piggy eyes off the girls doing handstands and showing their knickers with the other lasses with their skirts tucked into their knickers doing hopscotch. It must have been a pervs paradise just watching the lasses and it wasn't long before Radish and Whispering Jack were in full show off mode as Tez balled a fast one at me, and I took swipe and missed the ball. Radish and Whispering Jack burst out laughing taking the piss. "Fucking just look at that Radish," croaked Jack, "Play Cricket," he mocked us, "you're bloody clueless." And Whispering Jack sauntered across the road and snatched the bat out my hand. "Give it 'ere, I'll show ya how it's done." And cleverly hoping to catch the girls' attention he starts swishing the bat around like he's Freddie Truman taking the crease for England. He takes one minute to comb back his hair to cover his bald patch because now the girls are watching, and he's bent over, bat in hand and poised to slog the ball. "Come on then," Whispering Jack shouts at Tez, "give us ya best shot. Ready!" and Whispering Jack is stood there all poised and waiting to slog the ball down the street for a six. Now old Whispering Jack doesn't know it yet but he is about to get the shock of his life, and I go across the road to give Tez a nod and wink. If old Whispering Jack thinks he can make us look daft, he is in for one hell of a big surprise. And instead of slipping Whispering Jack a fast one with the tennis ball, Tez has exchanged it secretly for a HEAD BUSTING CRICKET CORKY BALL. "Right ya' bastard," Tez, whispers aloud, "Suck this one!!" and Tez takes a slow long walk backwards with his face set fiercely at his target across the road, who is still showing off confidently as Tez backs up all the way down a nearby back alley for the big run up. "Where's he gone?" squawks Whispering Jack.
"He's doing a run up." I shout back at him and Whispering Jack mockingly laughs will full bravado. "He'll fucking need it."
And suddenly Tez is coming full pelt like a bat out of hell from the shadows of the black alley way and launches the corky ball full

pelt across the road at Whispering Jack. Remember we used the tennis ball to play at night because it was white and we could see it. When this bolt from the blue came bombing across the road out the darkness, Old Whispering Jack did not know what hit him and all we heard was a big dull crack as he took a big one right full on the noggin, and Whispering Jack just seemed to freeze like a statue for a couple of seconds, sort of drunkenly opened his mouth to say something that would not come out, sort of smiled all daft at this nearby lass looking on, and then the lights suddenly went out, and Whispering Jack slowly keeled over like a sack of shit and hit the floor with a dumb thud.

"Why ya useless bastard!" said Radish cleverly walking up, "Ya fucking useless as them kids, ya bloody tart." Whispering Jack is not in the best of health to answer, as you will appreciate with concussion and probably a fractured scull just two of the medical issues he will wake up to. And Radish is now in a hurry to make his cricketing point and not forgetting of course to make a good impression on the watching lasses and he just snatches the bat out of Whispering Jack's hand laid out cold on the floor in LA LA land where the birds do twitter.

And so Radish walks over the crease like he has purpose and takes up a dramatic bent over cricket stance, his skinny arse in the air and bat raised at an angle in poised anticipation of slogging the ball over the roofs. Whilst he might think he is impressing the birds, he just looks like a church gargoyle who has fell of the roof waiting to take a shit. "Eh just a minute," he says at Tez, and before he takes his swipe, and without so much as an "Are you alright Jack?" he drags his buddy and fellow comrade Cavalier, Whispering Jack out the way with all the consideration of moving a bag of old rags and dumps his out cold body in the middle road, "You'll be alright there Jack, back in a minute. I'll just show these little bastards, who's the Daddy," and he winks with enthusiastic expectation at one of the watching lasses, "Back in a minute babes, just watch this." And Radish is back on his crease, bat in hand, with a grim evil look of determination in his face ensuring the girls can get a good view and swoon as their hero shows them how its done.

"Ready!" shouts Radish. "Give it ya best shot, 'cause this is going into the next street ya little bastards."

Tez bites his lip hard with grim determination, "Right then Radish, bite on this!!" he whispers, and he backs down the alley again for another big run up. A moment passes as Tez disappears into the dark alley.

"What's he waiting for?" Radish shouts across the road, and then suddenly Tez is coming out the back alley like the Cannon Ball Express and let's loose the corky ball straight at Radish. Now remember Radish is expecting a tennis ball and anyone who has whacked a cricket corky ball and held the bat loose will remember you get one hell of a sort of electric shock through your hands when you whack it, but alas it didn't get that far. Across the road Radish screams in panic and horror as the ball speeds towards him in a fatal path of deathly vengeance, and being an instinctive coward, he ducks and the ball whizzes straight over his head with the zing of a speeding bullet and there is a great big crash of breaking glass followed closely with one hell of big POP like noise, that was not unfamiliar to the sound of a television tube blowing up. The kids did not need telling twice and they all suddenly scattered like hornets after the nest has been kicked, and they are gone into nearby back alleys or bolted through their front doors as they detected that something was seriously amiss when the ball had crashed through Stuttering Joe's window and something mysterious had gone on with a big POP!

Radish is in daze and doesn't know what it is going on with the street suddenly empty of kids and deathly silent, with only the sound of Whispering Jack moaning on the floor like a drunken dosser, "What happened Radish?" says Whispering Jack all groggy and smiling like a nut job who doesn't know what day it is. "Is it time to get up yet? Are ya making a cup of tea Radish?" Yes, Whispering Jack is still on planet Zod.

And suddenly there is the sound of thunder as Stuttering Joe's front door crashes open and he falls out the door in his mucky string vest with baggy trousers held up by a big thick leather belt. He can hardly breath but is screaming and breathing FIRE and he's shouting at the top of voice as he emerges at his front door surrounded by blue smoky fumes coughing and spluttering up his guts. "Mmmmmmmmmm..me Fffffuckimg telly's been blown up." Now all the neighbors are out with the old bags in their hair curlers and dressing gowns, all Whooing and Ahrring. "What's happened Joe, are you alright luv? Sounded like an explosion?" Stuttering Joe is dumbfounded, dazed and confused.

"Fffffucked if I know," coughs a still shocked Joe, "I was just watching the end of Opportunity Knocks and sssssomething comes ccccrashing through the fffucking window and blows me telly up."

And as the smoke clears, there stood in the middle of the street is the solitary lonely, isolated figure of Radish right outside Stuttering Joe's house, looking as guilty as hell and HOLDING A CRICKET BAT. For Stuttering Joe, the jury was in, and as far as he was concerned the evidence is overwhelming. Radish is guilty. "Yyyyyyou aaaagain!! Ya big fffffucking lanky streak of useless piss. I should've ffffffffffucking known it. Last week it was mmmmme fffffucking front door on that motorbike, now you've just blown mmmmmee tttttelevsion up. Have you gggggggot something agggggggainst me? It's a fffffucking vendetta this is, in't it Radish?"

And the neighbours are giving it loads now. "Why ya big daft bastard Radish, ya want grow up, playing cricket at your age. Do you know what time it is? It's well gone ten o clock."

Radish is stood, gob wide open and stuck for words, "It wasn't me," Radish protests his innocence, "It was kids," he instantly dobbed us in.

Stuttering Joe is now off his starting blocks with the evil of vengeance in his face and snatches the cricket bat out of Radish's hand. "A fffffffuckinh liar as well as a vandal, bbbbblaming kids. What fffffucking kkkkids?" And Stuttering Joe waves the bat under Radish's nose, "wwwwwwhat's thissss then daft bastard, I know you've got horse teeth, you'll be ttttelling me next it's a fffffucking ttttooth ppppick." And with that, Stuttering Joe whacks Radish across the noggin with bat and Radish goes down like a good one and plays dead to avoid another cranial beating by Stuttering Joe and now us kids are coming out the alley ways playing all innocent. "What's going on Joe, have you killed Radish?"

"Kkkkkkilled him? I wish I ffffucking had. He's nnnever bbbbeen alive that daft Bastard. Hhhhhe's just blown up me telly and I was watching Hughie Green, and the fffffucking thing's on the never, never."

And suddenly Whispering Jack is coming round and struggling to his feet, "What's going on Joe?" he asked sort smiling like a daft lad but is really still seeing stars.

"Hey Joe," says Tez, "It was Whispering Jack was doing the bowling. We saw him Joe. It was Whispering Jack, he was the one who would've have smashed your window and he's drunk just look at him."

Joe glares at a half conscious smiling Whispering Jack who is still half on planet gaga, "Er what's up with Radish Joe?" says a groggy Whispering Jack looking down at the crumpled heap that is Radish and suddenly Stuttering Joe takes another swing and there is an other all mighty crack and Whispering Jack is back on the deck on horizontal hold star gazing again. For just one second his head pops up with eyes all glazed and a dizzy confused stare of a man not at all sure if he is in this world or the next, "Are ya making that tea Radish," was Whispering Jack's last words to the semi-conscious world and the lights suddenly went out again.

And gradually, as Marmaduke Street retired to the cosy world of their flea pits two local Hombres slumbered under the night skies, and tomorrow would be another day in history of The Street of Misfits, but heed not any concern for those illustrious legends of Radish and Whispering Jack as they will rise again in the face of adversity. And, undaunted by the fates of bad luck and misfortune, just like The Lone Ranger and Tonto they would live to ride another day in their endless search for nooky. "Heyo Silver Away!!" "Da, da,da, Tata dum, tata dum, tata dum, dum, dum, tada dum, tada dum tat dum, dum, dum....(If you don't get the previous line, it's the music from The Lone Ranger – you idiots!!)

And as our tales of this intrepid duo unfold, their search for some willing creature to plant their meat and two veg into would indeed come close to success, only to be vindictively sabotaged by two mischievous Hessle Road child hob goblins. Readers will have to stay tune for that episode in later chapters as our scribbles travel back in time and mosey on through those long since past days of the 1960s that will never come again. But it will be worth waiting for, we can assure you of that. But hold fast there readers, there are more ten gallon characters to come like you will not believe and more mischief and lots, lots more fun yet to be done.

Chapter Seven

Now in those days nearly every street down Hessle Road had a
family of real weirdoes and our street was no different. In fact,
weirdoes seemed to be everywhere in those days. Now whilst
you might think in all our descriptions so far, Marmaduke Street
had more than its fair share of mega weirdoes, but what we are
about to describe to you we can only describe as super weirdoes
and the Hergsons were such a family and they lived in the middle
of Marmaduke Street. Now all of you reading this book must have
at one time or another seen the comedy monster television series,
THE MUNSTERS or The ADAMS FAMILY. Well the Hergson family
was like a combination of the two rolled into one. And whilst they
could be funny, they also could be scary and on a night they even
seemed to have their own private bolt of lightening over the
house, and inside you would see lights flashing off and on with
shadowy figures going by windows upstairs and down. Of course
us local kids nicknamed them all according to the characters in
the Adams Family and The Munsters. There was Daddy Hergson
and was he one scary bloke or what. He was only small and
walked about with this hunched back and a massive thick bottom
lip that hung down almost to the bottom of his chin. He had this
scruffy unwashed long hair with a big baldhead in the middle that
he combed over in a sort of Author Scargill style. No you could
certainly not call Daddy Hergson a trendsetter of the 1960s, and
the only thing missing when you saw him walking the streets at
night was, him being chased by a load of Transylvanian villagers
carrying fire torches. In fact, he looked just like that evil bloke
Igor in all those black and white Frankenstein films that you
would watch on a late Friday night before you went to bed and
you would scare yourself stupid, take up a torch and put it on
under the covers. And you could guarantee one of your daft
brothers would start making ghosty noises to scare you to death.
Three other blokes and two women lived in the house and all
them were just as weird as Daddy Hergson. Mammy Hergson was
known to us kids as Mortisha and the one daughter who also lived
there we called nick named Valeria after the sexy monster women

in the film Carry On Screaming. And to tell you the truth if you could put aside the buck teeth, glaring eyes and permanent odd ball grin, she didn't have a bad body, and there were strong rumours that Radish and Whispering Jack had been sniffing out the possibilities but even Valeria had knocked them back and we are sure that Radish would not have felt out of place inside the Hergson house and would have made a magnificent addition to the household stuffed, mounted and propping up some corner of the room next to the Mummy case.

Since none of us kids ever got to know their real names and we never dared to ask, we nick named all of them according monster TV characters. One of the three older blokes in the house we called Uncle Fester because he always had this bald scabby head with half his black teeth missing and always glared at you on the rare times he was out in the daylight hours. The two other blokes who lived in the house we nick named Gomez and Lurch. And sometimes if you were kicking a ball around in the street and it went over their back wall, it would be a dare for one of us to go and ask for it back. And we would approach the front door all reluctant, and when you knocked at the door, a like loud hollow echo would seem to come from behind the door. They rarely answered the door but when they did, you would hear these great big stinking size twelve "plates of meat" slowly coming to the front door with a big clump with each step and before the door had opened, your imagination had run way with you and you would bolt in case you were dragged inside into the bowels of the Hergson's mysterious abode and never seen again.

Generally, though they kept themselves totally to themselves and you rarely saw them during the day, but you could certainly hear them on night as the most unusual noises and sounds emanated from their house into the street. All sorts of scary stories went around the street about them, and rumours were rife about what Daddy Hergson got up to with his two sons when nosey neighbours gossiped they had been walking or stalking the streets in the dark early hours, and when many a cat went missing you could guarantee that it was the Hergson's who got the blame. And when anything strange happened in the street, with all the doorstep wagging tongues in curlers and arms stoutly folded pointing the flying finger of accusation firmly in the direction of the strange nutters who dwelled at the house with no number on the door, it was always the Hergsons who got the blame.

And whilst sinister mystery and the smoke of dark rumour surrounded what went on inside the Hergson House, it would be left to inquisitive urgings of me and Tez to uncover the mysteries and lurking terror that resided therein. So cup your up ears closer readers and listen to our whispers, and those of a sickly disposition take care what is to be revealed in later chapters as sleep and a peaceful mind may elude you for the rest of your days. For our story will guide you to a slow terror that will awaken you to the depth of human depravity that will make your heart beat with each word that is written, and a brown tortoise head will squeeze out between your buttock as we will take you on an adventure to the dark side and deep into the hidden recesses behind the locked and guarded doors of the Hergson household. **BOO!!!!!!!** But that's for later.

We all loved old man Foxy and he was by far one of the real pearls of Marmaduke Street. Everybody and all us kids liked to call him Foxy because he actually looked just like his name. He was lean like a racing snake with sharp poker features and a long foxy nose and was always smiling to himself like he was a nut case. He was never ever seen without this big mucky overcoat on that was buttoned up and held together at the top with this massive safety pin, and equally always wore this spiv trilby hat with a red feather poking out the side. Foxy was what we called on Hessle Road, a Tatter, or as they called them down South, a Totter, a ragman without the luxury of a horse and cart which he compensated for by pushing everything he collected on this old pram. He was always trying to flog something that he had got cheap from Melville's salerooms down Coltman Street. Everywhere he went he pushed this rusty old pram usually with a broken television on it and he would always give you a furtive nod and wink and ask in a whisper, "Don't know anybody who wants a telly do you?" and "You haven't got a spare cig on you?" and he would mince off down the street pushing this pram with a telly on it with this big mental grin on his face. Foxy always had some scheme on the go for making a bob or two, only his schemes always seemed to go tits up big style and us kids would usually be the main reason. If there was one good thing about living in Marmaduke Street it was that there was just so much potential for mischief, fun and winding up stupid people.

Mucky Sid Potter or "Thick Sid the Dustbin Lid" as we kids called him lived down one of terraces at the top of Marmaduke Street, a few doors from away from Taffy Touchwood. Now Thick Sid didn't get his name for winning The Brain Of Britain, and in fact describing him as being as thick as two short planks, would have been a compliment for Sid, and not helping the situation was that he would walk about with this vacant expression that always seemed to have a smile on it, and many a time someone down the street would take acceptation to Thick Sid's permanent smile, thinking he was laughing at them and taking the piss, and sometimes if Thick Sid was passing Criterion and some drunk was coming out the door, we would whisper to the drunk, "Hey Mister that bloke's laughing at you." And the drunk would turn around see Thick Sid standing in front of him with this nut case smile on his face and one punch later, Thick Sid would be laid flat out on the pavement outside Criterion with little birds and stars flying around his head wondering if he had been struck by lightening. And being good Kids we would help Sid up and all groggy he would ask, "What happened mate?" still with this nutty smile on his face and we dust him down and get him on his feet, steady him up, and another drunk would come out of Criterion and again we whisper to the drunk, "Hey Mister that bloke's laughing at you." And the drunk would let loose and poor old Sid was again sprawled out kissing the pavement. So what with people around the street taking umbrage at this seeming piss taking smile on Sid's face, and us kids playing tricks on him, Sid spent an awful lot of time in the perpendicular position and apart from his smile, was always sporting a black eye or a fat lip and generally looked like he done ten rounds sparing with Mohamed Ali on one of Ali's good days. A good description of how Sid spent most his time would be if you remember those blow up toy punch bags of Yogie Bear from the 1950's, that you could punch and they would just pop upright again, well that was Sid, donk and back up again, donk and back up again.

There were so many characters and weirdoes that lived down Marmaduke Street the list really is really a long one. So having described the primary characters we will weave in the other characters as we tell our story and as we meet them.

There weren't many snappy dressers down our street unless your Missus was on the game, or they'd got the suite out of Isse Turner's pawn shop for a couple of days, at least until it was returned a few days later for another thirty bob. And Thick Sid also wasn't known for his sartorial elegance, and he used to have this habit of wearing his last month's dinner and tea stained trousers almost up to his chest with this great big mucky thick leather belt holding them up. Since he never worked, or likely never knew what the word "work" meant, he could usually be found at most times of the day leaning against his front garden gate in his grayish white, rarely washed, if ever, string vest drinking tea from a thick brown stained white tin rusty mug and taking in the gossip over the fence as the local fat fish wives stood, arms folded, hairs all trussed up in curlers and a housewife's turban and sporting the latest hot sexy fashion in white plastic fish house wellies with thick grey fisherman's socks half up to the knees.

That morning me, and Terry were going fishing on the Humber quayside next to St. Andrew dock, just behind the big stinky fish meal factory that use to stink Hessle Road out in those days. God that place used to stink. We were off to catch some eels that we could sell to the local wet fish shop. Eels were big sort of a big business in those days and today too I suppose. Blokes used to have eel nets all the way down the muddy Humber shoreline and when the tide was out, they used to empty them and the story went that the eels were shipped to London for the Cockneys who just loved jellied eels, YUK!! But how anyone could eat anything out of the Humber was beyond me, as in those days they used to pump raw shit into it and sometimes, if the tide was low enough you could see all the shit and piles of rubber Jonnies (Durex) pissing out of these big sewerage pipes that were dotted down the shore line, and strangely enough fishing near the shit pipes was usually a good spot for catching quite a few eels or flat fish.

So that morning there was me and Tez and we are trespassing in Taffy Touchwood overgrown jungle of a front garden digging for worms to use as bait. To get the most juiciest worms, what you would do is soak the ground the night before and that way the worms would be on the surface by the next day. So the night before we had spent a couple of hours quietly and sneakily throwing buckets of water over Taffy's front garden and pouring a couple through his front door letter box for good measure. Sounds daft when you think of it now, but we thought it was funny at the time, and that was just one of the less extreme mischief we did.

Anyway as we are digging up Taffy's front garden as you do, next door the two fat street gossiping gassers were out and giving it loads. Now lots of women were fat in those days but Sweaty Betty abused the privilege good and proper, yes she was one fat smelly fucker and that was the truth. Sweaty Betty and Flo were in full swing faces contorted and "Ooohing and ahrring" to each other over the front garden fence as they set about demolishing somebody's reputation.

It was really strange when you look back as all the women, especially the old bags, in those days always seemed to have their hair permanently in rollers and all trusted up in spotted factory turbans with full cover body piney on. And were they big women or what, and the were usually built like Hull FC prop forwards, and nearly always with legs rolled up in bandages and dark brown surgical stocking holding it all together with fish house wellies on and socks over the top. Yes, women in those days certainly cut fine figures of sartorial elegance, and yes I am being sarcastic and because most of them worked in fish houses as Patty Slappers, they always hummed like fuck of fish. Me and Tez often wondered how their husbands could shag such ugly gas bags, but I suppose if you are desperate and you have downed ten pints down your neck, as my mate Tez would say, "You don't look at the mantle piece when you're poking the fire" That was a big saying in those and when you've had a few, anything will do, even Sweaty Betty and Flo and Flo, who was also nicknamed locally as Flora, after the margarine, because according to local rumours she was always spreading her legs.

We could not help but overhear. Sweaty Betty was the Queen witch of the terrace was giving it loads to nosey old Flo. Locals joked that Florie wore braces on knickers because she dropped them so often it saved her having to pull them up. It wasn't long though before the lanky streak of piss, Taffy Touchwood came out telling us to clear off out of his garden. Taffy could be a bit of a scary character to us kids because he had this face with more holes in it than a pikelet long past its sell by date.
"Leave 'em alone ya' miserable old bastard." Sweaty Betty snorted at him, "They're only collecting worms."
Whilst old Taffy was one short of shilling he took shit off nobody.
"Mind ya' own fucking business you old bag and go get a bath. A fuckin' good bath would kill you!"
Yes, "Mucky bastard." "Go get a bath." "You fucking stink." And words and phrases of that ilk did seem the predominant insults in those days and thrown around with gay abandon and I suppose with good reason. But really when we think back none of us really had the right to call any body else a mucky bastard because nearly all of us were second to bonny in the personal hygiene department.

Now we are going to do something a bit novel here, and just for historical interest, and those interested in the sophisticated nature of the culture of the times down our street, me and my mate Terry quote here a small collection of insult gems from the

1960s Hessle Road abuse hit parade charts that were regularly thrown at each other during the regular set-toos, punch-ups and general bawdy carry-ons that went on down our street on the course of a normal days business as it were.

So let's have a drum roll and here we go pop pickers, as Alan Freeman would beat out on Sunday night, as he counted down the pop charts to us teenagers eagerly sitting around the coal fire on a cold Winter's Sunday night listening to the nicked tranni radio. "At number 8 it's…"

8. Sitting at number 8 it's…"Go home and clean your mucky house ya bastard!"…………..That was a popular one.

7.Climbing up one place to number 7 is…"Get in ya dirty bastard!"………………………………..A regular rejoin.

6. And down one this week, it's at number 6… "You want to try soap and water ya mucky bastard"…A very popular endearment we recall.

5. And hot on the heels at number 5 its…"Eye, at least our lass dun't drop her knickers like yours!" Often said about many.

4. And its still there at number 4 its…"At least my kids haven't got fleas and dicks like yours, mucky bastard!"…But they probably did.

3. And dropping back from number 2 is…"At least my house dun't stink!"…Now would be a lie.

2. And hoping for the number one spot its…"Who's ya fucking husband shagging now then!"………..Used liberally in those days.

1. But it's still there at number 1. Holding its place since 1945, yes it's…"You had a lovely bleedin' war, you did shagging all

them Yanks." ...Yes, often said about many. One Yank and your knickers were off!

Beep. Beep. Beep. "It's seven o'clock, and this is Allan "Fluff" Freeman signing off for another week of the Hessle Road Abuse Charts, so until next pop pickers. So see ya next week...Alright...Not 'arf"

Now after Allan Freeman's chart would finish at seven o'clock and your heart would sink as you would know what was coming on next, and you would hear that bleedin'awful seven o'clock, beep, beep, beep and... "Now here on Radio One we switch to Radio four for 'Sing Something Simple" featuring the Cliff Adams Singers, with Jack Emblow on accordion," and an angelic chorus would suddenly burst into heavenly song of, "Sing something simple, just you and I, sing some thing simple just you and I..." And as if a Sunday bloody Sunday, wasn't bad enough, it would be a real depressing downer after you'd been bopping away in some young lass's front parlor to strains of the top twenty and Fluff Freeman and suddenly DEATH is on the airwaves.

Sorry about that folks, me and Tea couldn't resist that one because we remembered that we all used to tune into Radio One on a dark winter's Sunday to listen to Fluff Freeman's chart show and just after Fluff Freeman had finished, that God awful chorus of... "Sing something simple." would cut in and someone in the house always shouted, "Turn that fucking shit off!!!"
The list of our chart of insults thrown around in our street is course not exclusive or exhaustive and we will certainly add more as they come to mind as our story progresses.

So back to Taffy Touchwood's front garden and we are just stood there in our usually mucky clothes with our arses hanging out the back, digging away minding our own business and ear wigging on Sweaty Betty and Flo, and we knew a good old Hessle Road barney was in the brewing here, so we weren't clearing off in a hurry and risk missing a good old punch up, no fuckin' chance.

Mind you old Taffy did have a point I must concede, because we didn't call her Sweaty Betty for no reason. Old Sweaty Betty had an exclusive perfume all of her own that was reminiscent of distilled fish meal, and was a characteristic stink of all those who shoveled fish meal at the factory on the docks where Sweaty Betty worked. Anyway Sweaty Betty's honor had been besmirched as it were by Taffy casting his abusive aspersions of laxity in personal and domestic hygiene department.

"Well I never," said Flo puckering up her lips all indignant and also determined to wind this episode to the next phase, "you're not going to take that fucking slather of him are ya' Betty?"

And with that Sweaty Betty rolled up her sleeves and humped up her more than ample bosom from round her knees. "Cheeky bastard, I fuckin' ain't," she shouted at the top of her voice, "We all know what you get up at night don't we, ya' dirty old bastard rubbing ya' self up against all them trees. Why, you need locking up ya' filthy swine?"

Over the garden gate Thick Sid is loving it, "Go on Betty luv," he shouts, "You fuckin' tell him."

"And I'll tell you something else Betty," says Flo, all flustered, "I've seen the way old Taffy looks at you when ya' walking down the terrace. I tell ya' Betty he's lusting after you. You can see it in those shifty little piggy eyes."

"My God a woman's not safe around him," announces Sweaty Betty aloud. "Now get in ya' dirty old bastard before my Bert comes out and give you what for."

"Well you go fetch him," Old Taffy challenges lunging at her over the fence.

"Oh my God," says Flo, "Did ya' see that, he tried to touch ya' Betty. Just think you could be coming home one dark night and he could be lurking in the shadows, drag you down an alley and have his wicked way with ya' before ya' could fart."

Sweaty Betty lunges back at old Taffy, "We'll fuckin' see what my Bert has to say about this." And with that Betty screams at the top of her voice like a strangled banshee, "Bert!!! GET YA' FUCKIN'

ARSE OUT HERE luv!!!" And that's Betty being romantic with Bert.

And with that call to arms Betty's beloved and faithful father of her children (he thinks) Bert, emerges out the front, and you've guessed it, in his string vest with baggy pants held up with the standard street issue black leather belt, and he storms out like a man with purpose, with all the poise and charisma of an Arthur Mallard lookalike. "What's all the fucking shouting about?"

"Him!" shouts Betty pointing at Taffy, "He's just called me a mucky bastard Bert!"

"I heard him too Bert," Flo puts her ten penneth in, "And he said a good bath would kill her. Disgusting he is." Flo looks at Taffy and turns up her nose like he is a bad smell.

With crocodile emotion in her voice and dabbing her eyes, "What your goanna do about it Bert?"

We have all stopped digging now and all stand there giggling under our breaths and Taffy is out his front gate and the string vest duo meet face to face over the front garden gate.

"And what you goanna do about it ya' fat bastard?" Taffy stares him down and the first punch is thrown as Taffy rocks Bert with a big right hand. "Go on Bert, stick one on him!!" we all shout and now punches are being thrown left right and center and the neighbours are out like it is fight night, drinking tea and eating toast. But it's old Taffy touchwood that's knocking seven bells out of fat Bert and Bert suddenly goes to return fire on Taffy, when Taffy lands a big one right in the guts that lands with and almighty thud and as Bert bends over in agony. Taffy then donks in blistering upper cut and Bert wobbles on his feet with eyes swiveling, and bang, he hits the deck in crumpled heap like a bag of rags and then Betty is on Taffy pulling his hair and landing big ones left right and center, "You Bastard, hit my Bert would ya!"

"Go on Betty!!," Flo shouts, "Hit him again!!"

Now in those days many women could give as good as they got and stand their corner in a fist fight, but sadly not poor old Betty, and not being the chivalrous type were woman were concerned, Taffy donked Betty right on the nose and when Taffy casually walked back into his garden, Betty had joined hubby Bert with legs sprawled apart showing all her gusset and was spark out cold in the land of nod atop of hubby fat Bert. It was a bit disappointing to tell you the truth, we were looking forward to, blood, snot and shit flying left right and center with blue lights speeding in from Gordon Street cop shop. But alas it was not to be and it was all over flash, and then Taffy turned on us and looked at us with a mad snarl in his voice. But before he could have a go at us, Tez pointed at Thick Sid still at his garden gate with that permanent Cheshire cat smile on his face and said, "Hey Taffy, Sid is laughing at you." With that Taffy quickly turned round and seeing Sid with his grin, goes over all angry and with a lightning right hook upper cut slugs Sid right in the mush as Sid is lifting his mug of tea to his mouth, and both Sid's NHS false teeth and his mug go flying into the air as does Sid, and he is lifted off the ground and lands with a thud out cold and still smiling, and with that Taffy, slapped his palms at a good job done and is now turning on us "And you lot can fuck of annall." And we didn't need telling twice, but we had enough worms anyway and it was left to the neighbours to pick up the untidy remains of Sweaty Betty, Bert and Thick Sid and cart them inside to lick their wounds having unsuccessfully cross swords with the legendary Taffy Touchwood of Marmaduke Street.

A real lot of people got the wrong idea about Taffy Touchwood and would pick on him thinking he couldn't fight and would end up like many, if not all who took him on, and laid in a crumbled heap on the floor staring up at the stars spinning around their head. But the characters in our street did make for a really interesting childhood and whilst we did wind them up for the chase, we got and equal amount of good pastings ourselves for the trouble. But a good hiding never seemed to stop us in our misguided search for fun, adventure and a little bit of danger as well.

Well now you've met some of the misfits of the Marmaduke Street of the 1960, but believe me and Tez there are more to come, many more and you will also meet again those already introduced to you as we weave them in and out of our kids' tales of times long gone from old Hessle Road.

Chapter Eight

Back to 2015 for a second

With me and Tez and our weekly, and increasingly daily meetings in the Avenue Pub playing over our old times as children down Hessle Road and turning them into historical scribbles of humour for those of our generation, we would always start with best intentions, but as the beer flowed we did tend to get bogged down with nostalgia. I suppose like most people of our age and experiences we hanker to go back, but we can't, so we just sit there, slinging the beer down our necks as we exchange memories and remind each other of the stories of mischief and fun laughing as we go. I mean non of us had a half penny to scratch our smelly arses with and it was hard for almost all the families down Hessle Road. I don't suppose you think about it at the time because you saw few who were any better off than you and there many who were worse off than you. I suppose it was all just relative and we just got on with it and never really thought about our lot, but, Oh what bloody good days.

Back to 1968

Now, because none of us had any money in those days as little poor kids. We were always in the game of looking for ways to earn money when we were kids, sometimes legal, sometimes not. But one story Terry reminded me of, was one money making stunt that went disastrously wrong, but not really for us, but for those living down Marmaduke Street. And by hell were we made to suffer for it and we might have got the pasting of our lives. But as the fates would have it, a dodgy knight in shining armour inadvertently came to our rescue, and instead of me and Tez getting the pasting, it would be some one else. And when you see how this pans, you will come that age old conclusion that greed and dishonesty has its own natural way of giving harsh punishments, and justice can sometimes be so fitting and so sweet for those little kids like us, that were often wronged and ripped off by grown ups.

But no getting away from it, now looking back, what we did was so bloody daft and only us could have thought we could have become millionaires from such a stupid idea as what we are about to narrate to you. But it turned out so funny. Our arses might have been sore for week from the consequences but it wasn't from a pasting, but that night we sat on the steps of Constable Street School, drinking a bottle of Hull Brewery mild we had bought from Bev's off license together with a packet of five Park Drive tipped and we just rolled about laughing at the day's events we now narrate to you. So here we go then.

So this day we are off fishing on the St. Andrews dock and I'm upstairs at home getting all togged up and me Mam shouts upstairs, "Ian your little friend's here," and, "I'm going to Carlines Supermarket shopping. Don't keep your friend waiting." Carlines in those days was like what the local Adsa supermarket is today but without cameras so you could nick loads of stuff.

"Ok Mam down in a minute!" I shouted back and I slogged on my shoes and thumped down the "apple and pairs" thinking Tezza is waiting for me, and who is sat in the back palour but Polo, and she's got that look on her little mischievous naughty devil face, and I could see she has come for another snogging session because she is sat all sprawled out with her gym slip up her legs with a flash of her knickers showing, and my eyes are popping out my head, "Hello Ian!" she says with one of her suggestive oozing stares and she is up and on me, "Give us a kiss Ian!"

"No!! I wont," I snap back at her fighting her off, but I can feel myself weakening already.

"Oh come on Ian," she says all girly and tempting. "Just a little snog." And she is already pressing on my leg like of them dirty old street dogs.

"No!" I snapped back again, trying to push her off, "cause you always want to do mucky stuff and me Mam will kill me if she finds out."

And then she smiles all tricky, "Well, what if I tell me Dad what you made me do?" and she is like threatening me, "And he'll come round and tell ya Mam."

"ME!! But I haven't done anything," I retorted, "It's you! You that does all that pressing stuff. And if you don't stop it Polo, I'm telling me Mam. I don't want to go blind."

Polo just gives a girly giggle in my face, "But what if I tell me Dad first, who do you think ya Mam will believe, eh Ian. I'm a girl, and everybody knows girls don't do mucky stuff. It's boys that do mucky stuff."

And thinking about it, she did have a point there, and me Mam would murder me. I remembered what Mam did to my older brother for taking lasses down back alleys after I told on him, so I could expect no help off him and I swallowed hard. "You won't do that will ya Polo? Me Mam will kill me!"

"Alright then," says Polo all cheeky, "But you'll have to trade something."

"You can have me catapult if you like," and she shakes her head. "Me pea shooter then?" And she shakes her head again. "What then?" as if I needed to ask. And without further a do, suddenly she is up and on me again and her face is almost stuck to mine with her lips sucking on me like a sink plunger. And I'm fighting her off, and she pulls me on the couch. "Polo Stop! Stop!" I'm protesting but have to admit my resistance is fading and I'm doing little to fight her off as other things are happening now. "Stop it Polo, we can't do a snog on me Mam's couch."

"Why not!" she argues back still pressing and snogging on me like one of those randy dogs that try and shag your leg.

"It's me Mam's couch that's why!" I struggled back with her lips still stuck to me. But it was futile and I just couldn't help myself and me and Polo are hot snogging and writhing away on me Mam's couch. The one she sits on and watches Coronation Street whilst puffing on a Park Drive and having a cuppa, and we are rolling all over doing our usual mucky routine until matters rise to there usual heavenly crescendo and me and Polo are suddenly laid out on the couch panting as the moment of urgency goes as quick as it came, and once again I am feeling even more ashamed of myself, as I have now just desecrated me Mam's couch. Polo was becoming like a bad habit, and whilst I tried desperately to resist her fatal charms, these odd urgings in the lower body regions, was where like lived a little devil monster inside me, and Polo knew just how to push all my buttons. I mean we didn't have sex or anything, not that I knew fully what sex was, but the hot snogging and pressing certainly seemed to do the trick just as good and whilst I was not sure what was going on during these moments of lost control, it was certainly very nice and I was always worried about me Mam finding out. And every time me and Polo had one of these sessions, I would swear blind and on a stack of bibles it would not happen again, but it always did and I just hated myself for it. And then to top it all, as Polo is dancing out the front door, having had her wicked way with me yet again, and who does she bump into but Tezza on the doorstep. He looks at me and shakes his head with disapproval, "At it again eh Ian?" "It's not me," I protest, "It's Polo, she won't leave me alone. But it won't happen again, I can tell you that Tez!" And I was determined but I think Tez had lost all faith in me by now and Tez just shakes his head, "You'll be for it Ian if ya Mam finds out," he said in a rising voice of like grown up disapproval. "And you'll go blind."

Now down our beloved Marmaduke Street, like a lot of streets on Hessle Road in them days, lots of people worked and lots of people didn't, and down our street we had more than our fair share of dossers that didn't. In those days people who had chosen the "sick" or the dole as a path career option were called dossers. There were called other things far too naughty to be mentioned in print, so dossers will have to do. Dossers used all sorts of excuses for not working in those days and they ranged from the legendary "glass back" to flat feet, and as me old Mum used to say about her brother, my Uncle Harold "The lazy bastard wants to get him self a job, never mind ten sessions a week propping up the fuckin bar in Criterion."

Yes, when me Mam was in a bad mood, Uncle Harold tended to get the broad side of Mam's tongue, and me Mam would rush about

the house cleaning and slagging off Uncle Harold under her breath as she went. And so she would rant on and dust around me and Tez like me wasn't there, just sitting in the back room watching Torchy the Battery Boy and quietly sharing a fag and me Mam is still ranting away to herself. "It's funny how our Harold's back dun't bother him when he's dipping his wick with her down Rosemond Street. The dirty bastard, that woman has had more pricks than an old dart board. He wants to watch himself does our Harold with her or he'll end up seeing the knob doctor. A hard day's work would kill our Harold. Ya poor old Granddad would turn in his grave if he knew how our Harold had turned out."
I don't know if me Mam loved her brother but I don't think Mum had much time for Uncle Harold. And I don't know why she always pretended Granddad was dead, when we all knew he lived in Grantham after doing five years on the Isle Weight in prison for bigamy with four women. Granddad was an Irish traveler you see and put it about rather a lot, and at the last count according Mam had more kids hidden away than Soft Tom and Casanova put together. So our Uncle Harold I suppose was doing no more than following in Granddad's footsteps as it were, and keeping up the family tradition as well as keeping other things up as well. Yes, our family certainly had a strange bloodline. Granddad an Irish traveler and me Dad was from Yemen, wherever that was. But me dad won't be featuring much in this pages as he is pushing up daisies across the oceans on some foreign shore somewhere. Or so me Mam says anyway.

But personally I didn't mind me Uncle Harold and he was always a good for a laugh if not much else, and so occasionally I would stick up for him when me Mam was giving him a good slagging. "But want Uncle Harold in the Army Mam fighting the Gerries Mam?" I would ask her.
"Is that what the lying lazy bastard told ya." Me Mam would say, "The nearest thing ya Uncle Harold got to fighting Germans was when that Krout seaman decked him out cold in Wassy Arms for mine sweeping his pint." No me Mam never had much of good word to say about me Uncle Harold.

For Dossers like me Uncle Harold, the major past time of the dosser was whiling away his long lonely days and the hard earned tax money of others slinging Hull Brewery mild down his neck, morning, noon and night at the local Hostelry de Marmaduke Street, otherwise known as The Criterion Pub on the corner of our street. For us kids, mainly me and Tez it was always worth a quick look in if we were passing, for a good old wind up and we would open the door because it was always the usual suspects propping up the bar boozing away their dole money or "sick" money endlessly while the grafters were out all day at the jam butty mines as it were. We would usually quickly open the door pop our little heads round and shout in chorus, "GET TO WORK YA' LAZY BASTARDS!" And then run like hell, as they would chase us down Hessle Road. Mind you if they caught up with you, you would get a good plastering, but most of them were so bleedin' lazy they'd just growl and get as far as the front door, and that was them done for the day. So they rarely got out the door to chase us, let alone catch us. Though one day Duckey Drake did give chase but ended up tripping over the front step outside the door of the pub, and cracked his nut on the pavement and ended up spread eagled outside the door out cold, with this glazed look on his face as he laid in the gutter and ended up getting carted off in a cop van for being drunk and disorderly. No poor old Duckey Drake never had much luck in life and the rumour was he was so ugly when he was born that the midwife, instead of slapping the baby's bottom, slapped his mother instead.

So anyway back to the story and some kids' mischief. We sneaked up to the pub front door and snook a look inside. It's all filled with thick foggy smelly fag smoke and I can see my Uncle Harold through the smoky mist, and as usual there he is, with that permanent roll up fag hanging from the corner of his mouth leaning on the bar trying to look down the front of Big Bertha the barmaids dress and giving her a chat up line. Mind you I didn't blame him for trying to get a butchers down Big Bertha blouse because she had these enormous tities like those girls in the middle page of that mucky magazine for grown ups, Parade. And Big Bertha was a bit of a show off and liked to show off her big boobies to all and sundry and for us little kids, who were always looking in dirty magazines and our big sisters' catalogues on the knickers pages at ladies titties, it was always worth a gander at the real McCoy.

Now for some unknown reason, my Uncle Harold has always fancied himself as a bit of a lad with the ladies. And God knows why, he had about as much charm and style as Albert Steptoe and was marginally better looking than Herman Munster on a good day and smelt worse than that French Loony Tunes cartoon character Pepi Le Pew. And Uncle Harold has got more chance of throwing his leg over the ragman's horse than throwing it over Big Bertha, though rumour had it many had, but unfortunately not my Uncle Harold.

Yes, Big Bertha the barmaid had a bit of reputation for being a bit of willy teaser, but many a night we'd spotted her down Jacklin's fish shop alley in the throws of passion, with her dress up around her neck and her knickers around her ankles, with a drunken fisher kid doing a limbo dance between her legs. But you have to give it to my Uncle Harold, credit where credit is due, he was a tryer and always a generous man on dole payday especially when he had a few. "Here luv," he says dragging an easy pound note out of the his arsehole pocket, "I'll have another pint and what do you want Luv." Big Betha smiles all brash across the bar, "Thanks Harold, I have a double vodka and coke I guess." My Uncle Harold almost chokes on his fag, "Well fuckin guess again and get yourself half a lager." And then he makes his big play to get into Bertha's bloomers and he gives her a flash line intimating he's a down on his luck as a wily seafaring Fisher Kid, "I'm out of a ship at the moment luv, but I could be sailing any day now darlin'. So this is ya one and only chance to come out wiv me tonight and then I'm sailing, and who knows where or when I'll be back, or if I'll be back. It's dangerous out there Bertha rolling about in the cold Icelandic waters."

"Oh Yeah," someone shouts with a big laugh, "Where's that Harold, Pickering Park rowing boats. COME IN NUMBER 15!!" And the whole pub bursts out laughing.

"Err Harold," some one else shouts taking the piss. "You being a seafaring man, you should know this."

"Try me," says Uncle Harold all clever and bullying himself up and hoping to impress Big Bertha with his nautical knowledge. "What did they call the ship in the film, MUTINY ON THE BOUNTY?" Uncle Harold goes all sour faced and is racking his brains, "Now don't tell me, I know this, I know this." And the pub just bursts into fits of laughter and Uncle Harold is clueless as to why.

Me and Tez are still at the door watching, "Uncle Harold!" I shout over, "Lend us two bob?"

Now in those days, it was a serious thing for kids even to be looking in the pub as grown ups saw it as a place where they could have some piece and refuge away from the kids and usually the nagging wife as well. "Bloody clear off," my Uncle Harold shouts back, "And bloody get off home before ya get my boot up ya arse. I'll be seeing ya mother about you, ya cheeky little bugger."

"You ttttttttttell 'em Harold," Stuttering Joe joins in, "Chchchchchcheeky little Bastard's." And adds, "It's them two that are always ppppplaying ffffff.ffff....ffffoot ball outside my house. Well sssssmash my windows and you'll be ppppppppaying for them."

Both my Uncle Harold and Stuttering Joe are well on their way to getting pissed out their heads and me Uncle Harold's empty pint pot is slammed on the bar after a big gulp, "Stick us another one in there Luv," and off he slopes and staggers off to the bogs for a slash and Big Bertha pulls him another and is off wiping the bar. Now Stuttering Joe has edged his way down to the end of bar following Big Bertha and nattering away and eye balling her knockers, and Uncle Harold's newly replenished pint is left unguarded. Terry nudges me, and as no one is looking we rush in, and I swig down half me Uncle Harold's pint and Terry swigs off the other half, and we are out the door unseen, and so we are outside and I am standing on Terry's shoulders looking in through

the pub windows for my Uncle Harold coming back. Stuttering
Joe has parked his arse back down the bar next to my Uncles
Harold's empty pint pot and Uncle Harold has staggered back
from the bogs. Old Stuttering Joe is smiling and talking to the
barmaid and we know there is going to be fireworks when me
Uncle Harold spots his glass empty. "Come on, come on Bertha,"
my Uncle Harold complains, "where's me pint?"
"Well I've just pulled ya one," she squawks.
 "What's going on? What's going on?" says Terry struggling to
balance me on his shoulders. "Uncle Harold is back." I say with a
big expectant smile. And I am giving Terry a running commentary
because we know when Uncle Harold finds his pint pot empty,
there is going to be big trouble in the taverna. Uncle Harold
looked all mystified at his empty pint and then at a smiling
Stuttering Joe next to him, and without so much as a bye your
leave, my Uncle Harold has found Stuttering Joe guilty of a
felonious assault on his pint and Uncle Harold let's off a big right
hook with a big clunk on Stuttering Joe's chin and Joe's eyes roll in
circle and, 'TIMBER' as Stuttering Joe keels over and hits the deck.
"Pinch my pint ya bastard would ya," Uncle Harold shouts down at
a Stuttering Joe who is away with the fairies, "Er Bertha put us
another one in there will ya."
Outside me and Terry are laughing so much I fall off his shoulders
and we are both in so much stitches of laughter that our stomachs
hurt.

Now there was two ways onto the fish docks in those days. One
was through the white painted under pass at the end of West
Dock Avenue, or over the fly over at the end of Subway Street.
And for us kids because we weren't allowed on the docks, it
meant trying to sneak past the two little copper's boxes that
protected each entrance and exit to the fishing docks and the
fishing docks led onto the Humber Key side or the wooden Jetty
where we would always go fishing. The coppers where posted
there because people who worked on the mile-long fish dock
stands were always trying to smuggle out stolen fish for a family
fry up or sell it cheap to the local fish and chip shops.

That day we chose to try and sneak onto the docks through the subway tunnel and as bad luck would have it, the copper we kids always called the "laughing Policeman" was on duty. We called him the laughing policeman because of the song, "The Laughing Policeman" because he looked just like the big fat clumsy bloke who sang it. Anyway he hated kids trying to get onto the docks and always gave a you a rasping clout around the lughole and massive boot up the arse if he caught you sneaking on. But never say never was the motto of most of us Hessle Road urchin kids in those days and we always had some trick up our sleeve to get him out the way. Just at the bottom of the tunnel there was a telephone box. Anyway me and Tez could see these two blokes talking and heading off the docks. One of the blokes was carrying this big black hold all and so we rang 999 and told the operator with handkerchief over the mouth piece and putting on a grown up voice just like in the movies. "This is an anonymous tip off lady. There is a big job on tonight at the fish docks. There'll be a bloke dressed in a big black mucky over coat, wearing a flat cap and muffler and carrying a big black hold all. He's nicked a load of cigs off the trawlers." The operator thanked us and when we looked across at the Police Box, the Laughing Policeman was answering his phone and we knew he was getting our tip-off. We hid behind the telephone box and watched as the copper came out of box and straight away eye balled the bloke talking with the big black hold- all and next thing you know, it's hook line and sinker and the copper shouts over the bloke with a vengeance and words are exchanged and next thing you know, the copper has made a grab for the hold-all and a scuffle is breaking out just like we thought. And whilst the copper has this bloke in a head lock and they are pushing and pulling each other all over the place just like in the wrestling at Madley Street baths on a Monday night, we dash past in the commotion. As we slink past we have a sneaky look back as this copper has just given this bloke a Big "Mick MacManus" fore arm smash and is laid across him on the floor looking for two falls, a knock out or a submission as Ken Walton at the ringside would say.

We used to play all sorts of tricks on the coppers patrolling the entrances to the fish docks to get past them. And sometimes we would just go to Wilkingson's fish house down Wassand street where Tez's cousin worked as a lorry driver and if he was going on the fish docks, we would hide under the smelly green tarpaulin covers they used for covering up the fish, and he would sneak us on the back of the lorry onto the docks. And just as we were going past the copper on the gates we would jump out and wave and laugh to him as we sped past him, and the copper would be jumping about in the road shaking his fist at us and we would stick two fingers up at him and pull our pants down, bend over and show him our bare arses.

Anyway we are on the docks now and sneaking across the lock gates like a couple of infantry soldiers under fire before we get clocked, but we are well clear of the coppers now and off we toddle and go fishing not at the wooden jetty but cross the narrow lock gates to the other side and then down the key side just behind the stinky fish meal factory, and we unpack all our gear.

Now as you've probably guessed we're not rich kids with all the fancy deep-sea rod and fancy high-speed reels, were you can cast out into the River Humber for miles it seemed like. All we have for fishing is two pathetic five bob a piece hand lines from Boyes. Not that we bought them, who could afford five bob in those days and yes I am sorry to say me and Tez nicked them along with a flask for some hot tea or Oxo, because sometimes with the constant Humber wind whistling up your jacksey, it could freeze the balls off a brass monkey on the key side, and sometimes we would just stay out all night fishing as lots of kids did in those days. But sob, sob, sorry about the thieving but we were poor kids and needs must, so when you've been there, then you can condemn us.

So we baited up our lines and after squeezing on the soggy slimy worms onto the fish hooks, ran out our fishing lines, and after swirling around our lines over head like a sling shot, we cast out the lead weighted lines as far as we could into the mucky grey Humber waters, tied off the lines and sat and waited. So we sit with backs against wall intently watching the fishing lines until you thought the line was moving. All the blokes and kids next to us with big smart rod and reels and are reeling in eels and flatties (flat fish) almost every other minute, but us, we didn't get a sniff of a fish. But we knew why, it was because they had rods and reels and we had hand lines and they could cast out further and they also had multiple hooks on their hook gear. But anyway we are not too disappointed as this old bloke who was reeling in eels like they are going out of fashion packs up, and to our amazement he gives us a bag full of eels he has caught and its full. We knew we could make at least ten bob off the wet fish man down Hessle Road and in those days ten bob was a lot of money for us kids. Now it's getting late and every body is packing up and it's getting dark but me and Tez are staying because we know after they have gone this is one of the best places to fish and only our lines are in the water now. An hour later and it almost pitch black on the quayside and out in the Humber it is full of ships with their lights on. We crack open the flask of Oxo and Terry cracks open a ten packet of Number 6 fags and we sit there drinking Oxo and blowing off the fags staring across the black Humber night and now the lights are on down the key side.

"Are you gonna sea then Ian when you leave school?" asked Tez.

"Yeah but I'm off big boating straight away." I answered. Just to put any readers straight, 'big boating' was the nick name for going in the merchant navy on cargo ships, as opposed to going on trawlers fishing. "You don't go anywhere on trawlers, just out fishing for three weeks and back again. That's boring. I want to go to foreign places."

There was another reason I didn't want to go on trawlers either, there was all sorts of rumours and old wives' tales that went on about what they did to galley boys on their first trip, and there was no way I was going to get a bottle of HP source shoved up my arse.

"You can't go big boating," says Tez, "Without doing twelve trips on trawlers. You gotta do ya time on trawlers first."

"Our kid didn't," I snapped back, "He went straight onto big boats. But he went to Graves End and did ten weeks to train as chef and that's what I'm doing. Fuck going on trawlers. Did you hear what happened to Ernie's brother Fred on his first trip? All he could hear all night on the top bunk was the cook wanking himself stupid every night. And one night he tried bumming Fred. No thanks!!" And that was the end of that conversation. No with all the funny goings on I heard about what went on onboard trawlers, you could count me out. Sod that for a game of soldiers.

Although we had a bag full of eels the old bloke gave us we still hadn't caught one eel or flattie our selves- flatties are flat fish and you can eat them but they taste like shit out the Humber. And so we are just about to pack up when along the key side comes the two night blackened silhouettes of these two blokes. One is dragging a rope walking along the key side and the other is pushing this old pram laden with several plastic buckets sitting on it. The two men stopped and started to pull the rope up. You could see what ever was on the end of the rope it was heavy, and by now me and Tez were intrigued and got up to watch what was happening. As the rope came up and out the water we saw it was attached to a big red meshed onion sack and it looked bulging with something, but what, we weren't sure.
"What ya doing Mister?" Tez asked them.
"Shrimping lad, shrimping," said the bloke pulling up the rope, and he pulled the onion sack onto the key side and emptied it and out poured all these mucky grey shrimps along with some black miniature spider crabs, which the bloke threw back. The shrimps were all jumping about on the key side; there was bloody tons of them.
Now me and Tez knew that you could eat shrimps because you could buy them for six pence a bag at the local wet fish shop on Hessle Road. But these shrimps didn't look like the shrimps we ate. They looked all brown and mucky and bit yucky to tell you the truth "What do you do with them mister?" I asked him.
"What do ya think daft lad?" answered the bloke all short and obvious, "We eat them."

"Eeeeeeh!!" me and Terry cringed, "Can you eat them, they look all brown and a bit shitty."

"Well they do now," said the bloke. "But what ya do is take them home and boil them up with a lot of salt and they'll go all pink like those one's in the wet fish shop. All shrimps look like this when they come out of the water." And bloke shoveled them up and put them into one of the four buckets on the pram the other bloke was pulling. When we looked at the other four buckets on the pram they were all over flowing and full of shrimps. Me and Terry looked at each, and the same light bulb had lit in both our heads, and the bells of the cash till were already ringing in our little brains, money! money! money! money! Yes, the green-eyed monster of greed shone in our eyes and after the blokes had walked away, Terry said suddenly in a big swooning breath "We could make a fortune."

The next morning, we are up early and at the wet fish shop selling the eels. The bloke weighs in the eels. "I'll give you 15 bob for the lot?"

"Make it a quid mister and it's a deal," says Tez.

"Come on Mister," I say, "Make it a quid, that's fair."

The wet fish man laughs, "I'll tell you what I'll do, seventeen and six and that's my last offer, take it or leave it."

"Done!" says Tez and we all shake hands and the bloke gives us our money. And just as we walk away, I slowly turn and ask, "Hey mister, how much do you buy your shrimps for."

"Why have you got some?" he asked smiling.

"Might have, it depends," Terry answered playing it canny.

"I'll tell you what I'll do then son," says the wet fish man, "You bring 'em in, if you've got some, I'll look at the quality and make you an offer."

This bloke wasn't going to tell us anything, but we did notice he was selling boiled shrimps at almost a bob a bag, and last week they had been six pence. And from what we saw on the pram last night that bloke had caught enough shrimps for hundreds of bags and then we could catch more and more and make a fortune. Me and Terry looked at each other; our eyes wide open with pure raw greed.

Down the road and we are talking all excited like the money is already in the bank. "Well," says Tez, "It's only a matter of boiling them up and we could sell them on our own and get bob a bag. We don't need to sell them to him do we."

"Yeah!" I said all enthusiastic and with a big greedy smile, "cut out the middle man and go door to door." And we went home back to Terry's house and drew up our business plan. I noticed in Terry's kitchen he had kept one big massive eel and had it swimming about in this big metal bucket. "What you kept that one for?" And I curled my face, "Eeeeh, you're not gonna eat it are you, it's been in the Humber swimming about in all that shit."

I knew people down in London like the cockneys loved their jellied eels but the thought just made me feel sick. I looked at Terry and cringed my face again, "Are you gonna eat it?"

Terry looked at me with one his faces and started sniggering and I knew some mischief was in the making.

Later that night we crept into Terry's garden and took out his Dad's ladders. It was about half past midnight and slowly and quietly me and Terry crept down Marmaduke Street in the dead of the night and down Sweaty Betty's Terrace. We also had this big massive black eel in a bucket. When we got down Sweaty Betty Terrace, our luck was in and we could see her front bedroom window was open. We snuck down the terrace like cat burglars in the night, put the ladders up against the Sweaty Betty's wall, and with Terry going up the ladders first with me behind carrying the bucket.

Now anybody who has handled eels out the River Humber will know that you just can't pick them up because they are so slimy and just slip through your hands and so you have to pick them up with a cloth rag and I we had forgot to bring a rag. Terry points to Thick Sid's washing hanging on the line and I climb down and take a pair of his, still yellow stained at front, under kegs, off the line and using them grab the eel out of the bucket and I'm silently up the ladders and passing Terry this massive ugly wriggling eel.

We could hear Sweaty Betty and Bert snoring and Terry quietly parted the curtains, and threw the eel through her bedroom window and we slid down the ladders like the wind.

"Just a minute," says Tez, and he still had hold of Thick Sid's underpants and they are covered in eel slime, and so Terry quickly slinks back into Thick Sid's garden and hangs them back on the line so that anyone who passes will see all the stains on them. "He'll have a hard time explaining them stains," laughs Tez and we're off to the corner of the terrace to wait for the explosion. We looked at each other quietly laughing, "I got it right on the bed," says Tez and we are both giggling. Then we counted down, five, four, three, two, one and lift off. An almighty blood-curdling Hammer House of Horror scream screeched into the silent night and lights were going on all over the terrace and neighbours were out in their curlers pyjamas all looking up at Sweaty Betty bedroom window as yet more screams bellowed across the terrace. Thick Sid, Mucky Mavis and "Spread 'Em Flo" are all out their front garden gates dramatically gassing and into Sweaty Betty's front garden and shouting up at the bedroom window.

"Are you alright Betty, what's Bert doing to you up there?" shouted Mavis. And then more screams.

"Give it a rest Bert ya dirty sod!" shouts Thick Sid.

"It's a big snake!!" Sweaty Betty's voice echoes out the window.

"What he doing to her up there." Mucky Mavis is now shouting.

"Leave her alone Bert ya dirty bastard." And Sweaty Betty is out her front door in her bloomers and short see-through nighty showing all the luscious body curves of a hippo, YUK! and screaming at the top her voice, "It's a snake, there's a snake in the bed!"

Me and Terry are listening around the terrace corner and creased up laughing and carrying the ladders we run back to Terry house with our sides aching.

Chapter Nine

The next day me and Terry were up early and had done a hot deal with old man Foxy to borrow his pram. Now old man Foxy is just like his name, a wily old Fox and he had guessed we were up to something dodgy. In fact, he was so interested in why we were so desperate to borrow his pram that we had stupidly let him in on our master plan with the shrimping and old man Foxy's eyes opened wide with pound signs on them, "I'll tell you what lads, I've got some buckets as well in the back," he said at us, with just a hint of something else on his mind. "Now then lads, this is the deal. I lend you my pram, and the buckets, and it's a three way split. Thirty percent each."

"Just a minute Foxy," I snapped back at him, "This was our idea." Old Man Foxy leaned at us all clever and smiled at us his with his gob full of blackened teeth and woodbine bobbing about in the corner of his mouth as he talked. "Yes, but you haven't got transport have you. It's me who's got a pram and you haven't got buckets either have you lads," and Foxy grinned with an evil Fagin-like face and he knew he had check mated us.

"So we do all the work and you get thirty percent." Terry sneered back at him, "On yer bike Foxy."

"Now fairs fair lads, and I'll even throw in the onion sack and the rope," said Foxy, "Now I can't say better than that can I now."

Me and Terry looked at each. "Just give us a minute Foxy," said Tez, "whilst me and my business partner here discuss it." And me and Tez retired around the corner and discussed our options.

"Look let's give him his 30 percent and on our way back we just drop a couple of buckets of shrimps off at my house." I said with a big smile. Terry laughed, "Course the silly old bastard won't be any the wiser." With our sneaky little devious plan all set to turn over old man Foxy we came back at him with our counter offer.

"Alright then Foxy," said Tez all fired up, "this is the deal Foxy, 25% and we do all the boiling up at your house."

"Boiling up?" said Foxy all mystified, 'What boiling up?"

"We gotta cook them ain't we," said Terry obviously.

"Mmmm," Foxy mumbled stroking his stubbly chin thoughtfully and then looked at us all eagle eyed, "If ya using my gas and electricity, it's thirty percent and you have a deal."

Tez looked at me and I looked at Tez and we both nodded our heads in agreement. "Alright," said Tez, "Thirty percent it is."

"Right what time we off then," said Foxy all excited.

"We'll be at your house after school." I said at Foxy all determined, "So make sure you've got everything ready."

"Don't worry," says Foxy, "I'll be ready, and don't even think of double crossing me, or there'll trouble," and he winked at us. "Get my drift lads?"

"What, you think we'd fiddle ya?" said Tez, slightly outraged.

"Money does strange things to people," said Foxy giving us the evil eye. "Don't worry Foxy, we'll come straight back to yours." I said reassuring him.

Foxy laughed all clever like, "Now you wouldn't be thinking of dropping off a couple of buckets of shrimps before ya get to my house would ya lads?"

"You know Foxy, you haven't half got an evil mind," I said all innocent, "cause we wouldn't." And I turned to Tez giving him a quick wink, "would we Tez?"

"We're not like that Foxy!" said Terry so stoutly he almost had me fooled. And we stared at Foxy like butter wouldn't melt in our mouths.

A big grin suddenly spread across Foxy's face, "Well that's alright then. You won't mind if I come with you then lads will ya." And Foxy stared at us like he knew what we planned, "Just to look after my investment like."

Me and Tez looked at each other and curled our lips. Foxy was one dodgy bugger and we would have to watch him carefully, very carefully.

After scrambling down eggs and chips for tea and I'm all excited at the thought of a making a bundle from our new venture and I can't wait, and I bolted from the table, "And where's secret Sam off tonight?" said me Mam at me. "Seeing ya little girlfriend?" she teased me. "She seems a nice little girl."

"She's not me girlfriend!" I snap back.

"Well who is she then," says Mam, "if she's not ya girl friend?"

"She's not me soppy girlfriend!" I shouted back sullenly, "She's just a girl! That's all!"

"Well pardon me for speaking, and don't be in late then, and leave us a couple of cigs," me Mam shouts after me, "Haven't got any," I shout back and I'm already out the the door and I've nicked my big brother Colin's Parker overcoat and I'm all togged up like Nanook of the North 'cause we gonna be out after dark and its cold out there on the docks at that time of night.

I was a man on a mission tonight and was already mentally counting the cash that would be rolling in. Nothing would stand in my way, or so I thought. But just as I'm passing Polo's house and she starts knocking on the window, and she has that naughty look of hot school girly passion on her face that always get my motor running, "Me Mam and Dad's gone out to bingo!" she shouts suggestively at me. And I give her a definite and emphatic shake of the head- 'Not tonight Josephine' But she always does it dun't she and she climbs up on chair in the window and pulls up her girly school gym slip skirt so I can see her little red school knickers, and she has this cheeky little smile on her face that promises more pleasures to come if I venture inside. And now I am weakening 'cause, naughty little mucky boy thoughts are going through my naughty mucky little boy's brain and my hormones are on full throttle and without hardly knowing it, like this big invisible magnet has pulled me through her front door, and the next we are on the couch snogging each others faces off. But as fast as the passions rise in young loins and after a bit of pressing and hot wrestling on the couch and we are both quickly satisfied and I say a big heavy, "Phew!!" and we both roll onto the floor staring at the ceiling. The urging fires of raging school boy and school girlie lust have now gone quickly out and I curse myself for letting Polo again catch me off guard, and I'm back out the door as quick I came leaving Polo laid on the floor taking in the moment of heavenly bliss as her animal urgings too were now as well satisfied as mine. And for the umpteenth time, I promised myself it would not happen again, but knew once Polo showed me her knickers; I would always be putty in her hands and a little boy not in control. Yes, I definitely needed to grow up and get my little one-track mind on other things and I was now very worried about going blind.

I meet Tezza, fifteen minutes late at the corner of Foxy's terrace and he's definitely not best pleased. He too is all done up like Eskimo Nell for the cold night ahead, with his old man's duffle coat on that is about six sizes too big for him, and underneath a polo necked sweater nicked out his big brother Allan's wardrobe, with a big thick balaclava covering almost all his head and face with just his beady eyes staring at me like one of those Zombie monsters on the midnight movie. We've also got a backpack with a flask of hot Oxo and half a loaf of bread for sloppy dunking. I try and make a joke and distract Tez from giving me an ear bashing for being late. "What do you call a German with sixteen Balaclavas on...anything you want, he wont hear you." But it won't wash and Tez is not best pleased as he has likely guessed where I have been.
"Where the bloody 'ell have you been," Tez snaps at me, "It's freezing out here and I bet you you've been tapping up Polo again. I thought you said you were giving her up? You just can't leave her alone can you."
"I try Tez, honest I do," I answered pathetically, "But she knows just how to get me going, and I just can't resist once she shows me her red knickers."
"You've got to stop it Ian, it is effecting business now," says Tez all grown up like. And he gives me another warning, "You'll go blind. And what if ya Mam finds out."
"It's definitely the last time mate, I promise." And I am determined. "Polo is definitely getting the big heave ho Tez, cross my heart and hope to die."
I could see from Tez's expression of disapproval he had little faith I could resist the delights Polo was always flashing at me through her window, and who could blame him. I was a big disappointment to myself. When it came to Polo, just one flash of her knickers and I was like a little boy in a trance just like those

Bisto Kids floating in on the gravy fumes, and then they were these mysterious urging I didn't quite understand that would take total control of me, and I always regretted it afterwards, but not for long until me and Polo were at it again, snogging, with her doing all this mucky pressing stuff on me.

So, Foxy pops his head out the front door, "Come you two lazy bastards." And he beckons us to come in. Now we'd never been in Foxy's house before and all that we knew about it was the street rumours and dark mystery not unlike what you'd hear about Dracula's Castle and it was a rude awakening to say the least. And as we went in the front door it smelt like one of them old people homes where they piss all over the place and the smell knocks you over at the front door. It was all dark and dingy and it absolutely stunk to high heaven. Me and Tez looked at each other and cringed. "Pheooooow!!" Tez whispered.
Old man Foxy was one hell of a hoarder and there was stuff piled all over the place and he had loads of those old wind-up gramophones record players with those big like shell horns where the sound came out of. And everywhere there was Second World War stuff like loads of old gas masks, German and British soldier helmets. "Core! Look this Tez," I said putting on one of the gas masks and a Gerry Helmet and Tez put on a British Helmet. "This'll be great for playing Krouts and British," says Tez, "Have you got any real guns Foxy?"
"Just you two be careful with that stuff," says Foxy all serious, "ya never know when we'll need it again. We might have to stick it up them Ruskies yet. Now take it off, unless ya buying."
"Oh come on Foxy, let me keep this." I say all muffled and echoe sounding because I'm still wearing the gas mask and lift up the gas mask. "Eh these really work," I said to Tez, "You can't smell Foxy's stinking house one bit," I whispered and Tez puts a gas mask on, "Oh Yeah," says Tez all muffled and hollow. "I can't smell a thing."
"Will you two stop mucking about," says Foxy getting all-irate, "we've got serious work to do." And so we took off the gas masks and helmets and again the stink of Foxy's house hit us and we

both cringed at each other and giggled and both decided we'd nick the helmets and gas masks later as they would be great for mischief in the street especially at night, knocking on doors and looking in windows you could scare people to death.

And there was more stuff everywhere we looked as we took a shufty around. It was like one of them old junk shops with masses of old televisions piled on top of each other everywhere. And in the eerie back room it was really scary and only the light of a candle flickered shadows across the walls and suddenly me and Tez jumped out of skins as Foxy had this old giant stuffed bear bearing its claws stuck standing in the corner with a big fierce look on its face that made me and Tez start to run for it and Foxy started laughing. "Don't worry he won't hurt ya. Not unless he falls on ya. I got him cheap off Percy the ragman. I was gonna make a killing but the bottom fell out of giant stuffed Russian bears. Ya don't want buy it do you?"

Terry laughs, "I suppose it could be interesting taking him Guy Fawking. But I fink we'll pass on that one Foxy."

"Eh Foxy," I say all excited, "Can we borrow him?'

"What for?" says Foxy.

"We could put it outside Stuttering Joe's door and play knock off Ginger." We all started laughing, "Old Joe 'ell have an heart attack." says Tez.

"I can do you a good deal lads, ten bob and it's yours," says Foxy.

"TEN BOB!!" retorted Tez, "We aren't got half a penny to scratch our arses."

"Suit ya self," says Foxy, "but if ya know anybody who wants a stuffed giant Russian bear, be sure to let me know and I'll cut you a couple of bob."

Me and Tez looked at each other, rolled our eyes and gave Foxy the thumbs up. "We'll ask about Foxy but I don't think we'll get killed in the rush."

"What about Tiger then?" says Foxy, "I've got full size stuffed Indian Tiger in the bedroom upstairs. Go real nice in your Mam's living room Coxy next to one of those stand up lamps."

We both shook our heads at Foxy, "What about a buffalo then?" said Foxy, half excited.

"A buffalo?" I retorted. "Where'd you get a stuffed buffalo?"
Foxy seemed to grimace a sour face, "Percy the Ragman, bought
the whole job lot of him ten years ago. The bastard said they were
coming back in fashion. That's what the smell is, that bear stinks
when it gets hot in here. I'm sure he hasn't been stuffed properly
and they've left a big giant Russian bear turd inside him."
It's all very interesting Foxy," says Tez, "But can we crack on.
Where's the gear."
"It's in the back outside," says Foxy, "But I've just got to hide me
money, ya know what the thieving bastards are like round here."
And he tells us to turn round and not look where he's hiding it.
But we both peak a quick look and old man Foxy has this money
belt on and we see him pull out this cash and roll it up and put it
in this bag. And then Foxy shoves this small bag of cash up the
Bear's arse with big efforted grunt. "Ya' can turn round now you
two." And he gives us this sniggering grin. "Not that I don't trust
you lads like, it's just me holiday money. Me and our lass are
doing a week in Hornsea and a week in Withernsea next year. We
like our travelling to different exotic places."
And so Foxy leads us into the back yard and there ready and
waiting is the pride of Foxy's transport fleet, his pram with pile of
six plastic buckets and top and Foxy had made up the onion sack
just right with the open end made open and rigid with a metal
frame and a long rope tied to it.
Me and Tez look at each other with big greedy grins and we are
counting our chickens before they hatch. "We're in business!" I
say to Tez, we spit on our hands and shake hands giggling like a
couple of daft lads on a day out at the loony bin. "Right," says
Foxy, "Let's go."
And off we charge into a cold Hessle Road night, me and Tez
pushing the pram and old man Foxy mincing along side of us in a
penguin waddle just like that spiv in the original St Trinians films.
We didn't know it at the time but we must have looked like a right
set of odd looking tossers as the night blackened silhouetted trio
of two little kids dressed up like German soldiers on the Russian
front with 'Heir Colonel' Foxy leading us into battle.

Foxy never told us he had bad legs and we had only got half way down Wassand Street across from Marmaduke Street and Old Foxy was huffing and chuffing and like an old Rag Mans horse and started feeling his heart. "What's up Foxy?" says Tez.

"It's me heart lads," taking deep breaths, "I'll never make it, and me legs. It's an old war wound. Got it taking out a German machine gun nest when we landed at Anzio," he said all forlorn and pitiful. "I still have nightmares."

"Anzio, that was a film with Robert Mitchem that was," I said, "The Battle for Anzio we sneaked in Cecil Picture House, me and Tez last month."

"Fancy you being there Foxy, did you meet Robert Mitchem then Foxy?" says Tez, taking the piss. And we start sniggering because we know the only war record Foxy has, is Vera Lynne singing, 'We'll meet again.'

"I'll get in the pram lads." And just like that Foxy climbed on top of the pram and me and Tez had to pull the pram like two Husky dogs, with him on it down Wassand Street, across the bombed buildings and down English Street to where there was a big hole in the railway walls down the dark, spooky and dingy Long Lane. Long Lane was eerie place even during the day that ran along side the dock railway lines and it was like a big dare on Hessle Road to go there at night. You could get to it if you went over the Stricky bridge at the end of Strickland Street and once over the bridge there was a long windy wooden stair case that went down onto the lane. But there was no way we could get the pram over the bridge and so we took a short cut route down English Street that led onto the lane. On a night it was pitch black down Long Lane and a real scary place with all sorts of rumours and ghost stories about a bloke called 'One Arm Nellie' who was supposed to haunt the lane after his arm was ripped off by train whilst trying to nick some coal.

Now there was a funny thing about the wall next to the railway line down Long Lane on the back of English Street, and that was, it was about four foot high on one side, but on the railway side, it had an embankment drop of about forty feet down this very steep slope that led onto the railway lines. It had caught out many a burglar after making a bolt for it running from the coppers as they had speedily jumped over the wall only to be met with this forty feet drop into oblivion on the other side.

So all we had to do after getting through the hole in the wall was then just to get down this steep embankment, across the railway lines and onto the cargo docks and then back up towards St Andrew's fish dock and the causeway behind the Hull Fish Meal factory. It was clear of coppers on a night but apart from the hole in the wall, the gates would be locked and it was the only way to sneak onto the docks. We must have looked a pretty dodgy sight sneaking about down Long Lane in the night blackness with our silhouettes pushing this old boneshaker pram down the road with Old Man Foxy sprawled on the top of it like an old Guy Fawks. By the time we got there me and Tez were knackered and sat down gasping for air just outside the hole in the wall and Foxy is sat on pram puffing on a Woodbine. "Come on lads, we're almost there."

"If you think we're pushing you over them railway lines," I protested loudly, "you've got another thing coming."

"Your kidding Foxy," Tez piped up all breathless.

"You kids today," Foxy scorned us, "You've got no staying power. I was only a few years older than you two when I was up to my neck in muck and bullets sticking it up the Gerries on the Beeches at Dunkirk."

"Was you really in the war then Foxy?" I said sniggering.

Foxy took on all insulted. "Course I was in the war! I've got a medal to prove it. I was on the front line in France when the first shot was fired."

Me and Tez was laughing now, "And back in Hull when the second shot was fired eh Foxy," said Tez taking the piss.

"Taking the bleedin' piss again," said Foxy sneering, "You two never give it a rest do ya. Anyway come on, let's get moving."

And so we both got up, took another heavy breath and started to push the pram through the gap in the wall and onto the railway. Now remember it's totally black and with no lights we couldn't see a thing and in the pitch black dark, we totally forgot about the big drop embankment on the other side, and all we knew next, is the pram had slipped our grasp, and with Foxy on it, was speeding down the night blackened embankment at a fair few speed of knots I would say, with Foxy and all the gear on it jibbering and rattling away on the difficult journey south. And all we could hear was Foxy screaming for grim death as he travelled down the embankment gathering speed and with a tail wind as well, how's that for luck, or bad luck even. Now we can't see Foxy because it is so dark and there are no lights any where on the embankment, but both me and Tez gathered from his screams Old Man Foxy was not much enjoying the ride. And the blood curdling nature of his banshee screams were more in keeping with a man who knows he is in great difficulty and focusing his mind on the great deal of suffering and pain that was to come at this, unplanned for journey's end of great speed. Foxy seemed to be traveling so fast down that embankment that I half expected to hear one of those sonic booms you get when a jet fighter goes through the sound barrier. But no, only screams of severe distress could be heard across those silent railway lines echoing in the otherwise silent and tranquil night. I tried at that point to put myself in Foxy's place, and I knew I would be thinking this is not going to end well. I think taking into account Foxy current dire situation, that, all in all he would be right on that one. And you know what, they say great minds think alike, and that's exactly what Tez was thinking funnily enough. In't that strange eh? Well we wanted to help but what could we do? As they say, the outcome was in the lap of the Gods now. I mean it was no use all of us panicking. In situations like this, some one has to keep their head cool, and so me and Tez got out the Number 6 tipped and lit two fags patiently waiting for the inevitable conclusions of this difficult event to play out and hoping minimum damage would be done to the equipment.

And then suddenly the screaming stopped, we assume as the pram came to a sudden halt as it hit the railway line at terminal velocity with a great metallic crunch, and in the dark all we saw was this black arm waving silhouette of Foxy flying through like the human cannon ball and to tell you the truth, and I know this is an odd time to think about it, but I was reminded of that old time musical hall song as Foxy's black silhouette flew through the air in like slow motion, "He flies through the air with the greatest of ease, that daring young man on the flying trapeze..." And then suddenly Foxy's black outline sort of stops for a second in the night sky, and then suddenly is starting in a downwards trajectory and goes off visual radar as the natural effects of gravity took over, and he disappeared from observation crash landing with a loud dull thump that made me and Tez grimace, as it sounded a somewhat painful landing. And I thought I saw a puff of what looked like black dust mushroom rise into the air. Now me and Tez weren't panicking or anything but we did scramble down the embankment in a hurry in search of Foxy's bodily remains in the dark, and we just followed the direction of the labored moaning and groaning of a soul in pain. We found the pram first and thankfully all the gear and pram was in tact, but strangely there was no sign of Foxy and no sound either. "You don't think he's dead do you?" said Tez all worried, and then suddenly we heard the sound of more groaning and slowly crept our way across the pitch black railway lines towards the groaning. But when we got there, there was nothing there but this big pile of cinders and ash were the steam trains emptied and cleaned their boilers. And then suddenly, as our eyes became accustomed to the dark, this pile of ash and cinders started moving and out popped Foxy's head first and still wearing his Trilby. And then slowly but surely, and some what disorientated, and covered from head to toe in black soot and ash Foxy emerged. Me and Tez tried not to laugh as Foxy looked like the monster from the Black Lagoon. "Don't just stand there like a pair of daft twats," shouts Foxy, "Give us a hand." And he's trying to get the soot out of his eyes. And suddenly we can see Foxy full on and we both just burst out laughing. "You look like one of them Black and White Minstrels Foxy," says Tez creased up.

"You two could've killed me," retorted Foxy all serious, "It's not funny!"

Now I'm all creased up and can't get a grip. "Eh Foxy, you must have travelled about thirty feet after you hit the line. You looked like Batman flying through the air. At least you landed on something soft."

"When you've finished taking the piss," snapped Foxy not at all amused, "Pull me outa here. Something doesn't smell right, I think somebody's had a shit in here."

And so we help drag Foxy out the cinder and soot mountain and suddenly me and Tez can smell it too and we both cringe.

"You know Foxy," says Tez, holding his nose. "I think you're right. Some body has had a shit in there."

"Smells like cat shit to me," says Tez having a sniff like one of those Red Indian scouts.

"Could be dog shit," And I have a sniff of Foxy, "Phew, smells like dog shit to me."

And Foxy then loses it. "Do you two want a thick ear? Are you two fuckin' daft or what!" he shouts at us, "What does it matter who's shit it is, shit's shit."

"There no need to take on so Foxy," I said at him, "I mean if it's dog shit or cat shit, you could catch something."

"Thank you Doctor fuckin' Doolittle," says Foxy as he starts to get up.

And I back away the stink is that bad, and I cringe "God Foxy you bleedin' stink!"

"Yes, I know I stink," he says all catty and matter of fact, "Cause you two toss pots you two have just launched half way across Hull into a pile of shit. Are you two trying to kill me or what?"

"It was an accident Foxy," Tez argued back, "Don't take on so. Ya like a bloody old woman Foxy! It could have been worse, at least the pram's alright."

And Foxy looks at us with a face that seems to lack a certain confidence. "Why do I have a bad feeling about this caper?" And Foxy steadies himself to his feet, makes a feeble attempt to dust himself down and in the process we get a full throttle sniff now Foxy is close up and personal, and me and Tez cringe our face like we've eaten a real sour apple. "Phewo. Foxy you don't half bleedin' stink," I said holding my nose.

"Yeah says Foxy," all sarcastic, "Sort'a reminds me of your house."

Foxy shrugged his shoulders with hard face, "Well you'll just have to get use to it won't you, because we've got a long night ahead of us."

And with that, he turns his nose up at us all snobby like and saunters off into the night across the tracks. Me and Tez get the pram and follow Foxy onto the docks giggling like daft lads as we are now getting the worst of the stink because we are down wind of Foxy.

Chapter Ten

Once we'd sneaked down the cargo docks on Albert Dock we crept like little war time commandoes silently then onto St Andrew's fish docks and cut across the lock gates behind the Lord Line building and broke camp at the back of the Hull Fish Meal factory where the long concrete causeway is and we dished out the shrimping gear. The Humber wind was blowing up real cold and in our faces and it was freezing and what with the stink from the fishmeal factory and Foxy it was going to be a long hard smelly night. We couldn't see out much into the Humber but we could hear the watery slosh of the sewer shit pipe that stuck out the concrete causeway wall just below us pumping out great waterfalls of Hull turds into the Humber by the thousand with more stink coming up out the Humber. Foxy was looking down at the pipe and cringing, "I wouldn't fancy falling in that lot," he says aloud, "Just look at it. You've got turds, rubber Johnnies and fanny rags. What do the mucky bastard's flush down their bogs. It's disgusting."

"Never mind that Foxy," I said at him. "You push the pram and me and Tez will pull the net." And so we dunked the onion sack into the dark brown yucky Humber waters and started pulling it along the causeway, and it was getting heavier and heavier as we walked and pulled.

"Pull it up!! Pull it up!!" shouts Foxy getting all excited and so me and Tez heaved and heaved, until the sack broke the water and Foxy was looking down, "It's bulging lads, it's bulging!"

"Well give us a bleedin' hand then it's heavy," grunted Tez pulling on the rope and now all three of are pulling up the onion sack. Suddenly its on the ground and we tip out the contents and a massive stack of mucky grey coloured shrimps pour onto the concrete jumping about all over the place along a with some black spider crabs that we threw back.

Foxy cannot believe his eyes and he looks like one of them old Wild West Gold prospectors who has just struck gold and laughing to himself like a nutter with gold fever. "Quick get the buckets, get the buckets!" he says laughing to himself and me and

Tez are looking at each other, as we've never seen old Foxy like this. So we shovel the shrimps up and into the buckets and we're off again dragging the net down the causeway, and we are hitting the jackpot every time with a full sack of shrimps and in no time all the buckets are brimming out the gunnels with the shrimps and the pram is getting heavier and heavier and harder and harder to pull for old man Foxy. By this time, me and Tez are exhausted but we are still pulling the sack for the last trawl. Time seemed to go so quickly and two or three hours just whizzed by and me and Tez were by now exhausted.

"I think we've got enough now Foxy," I said panting and pulling and by now we have pulled our way back to near the big shit pipe but it's stopped flushing now. The shrimp net is now so heavy and we are so knackered that we can't pull it up and me and Tez fall down for a breather all exhausted still holding onto the rope and prop ourselves up against the Fish Meal factory wall trying to catch a breather. Foxy is coming up close behind pushing the pram. It's now so dark we can hardly see each other and Foxy sees us sat down, leaves the pram and is just mincing up to us, and for the first time tonight me and Tez are pleased with our night's work, and Foxy as well for the first time tonight also looks like a happy man.

"Well that's it then lads," announces Foxy with a big happy grin. "Just get this one up and in the bucket and it's home time." And Foxy greedily rubs his hands does this little mischievous fairy dance, "Just count the money then, eh lads," he says with a snigger.

I was still knackered and so was Tez. "Well I'm glad we've finished." I said all cautious, "I was getting a little worried about the bad luck."

"Yeah Foxy," says Tez with the same ominous tones in his voice, "Me too. Ya know what they say Foxy, disasters always come in threes."

Foxy is confidently giggling to himself now, "Ah you two worry too much," retorts Foxy all brash and confident and gives us a quick lesson in the secret of his "success" in life. "In business ya got'a take risk," says Foxy, "That's just me, the way I am. I mean look how successful me telly business is."

"Just a minute Foxy," I interrupted him taking umbrage, "This was me and Tez's idea, and you muscled in."

"Yeah," says Foxy cleverly, "but who provided the backing. It's my pram, my buckets and my shrimping net."

"Don't you be getting any ideas Foxy about ripping us off Foxy," Terry announces, "cause our kid will knock ya head off."

"Yeah," I interrupted, "don't get greedy Foxy. Greed always brings bad luck. We could have a good thing going here."

And Foxy suddenly smiles at us, "Calm down lads, calm down. Nobody's ripping anybody off." And he starts laughing, "You two are always going on about bad luck. We've finished," he announces, with a hearty slap of his hands, "Let's get packed up and get boiling up. And stop being so superstitious. I mean what can go wrong now?" And with that Foxy steps back into the darkness to collect up the gear, and suddenly we hear this scuffle in the darkness, like someone tripping over a rope, someone screams in the night and Foxy disappears over the quayside and into the black Humber with a big scream and a great big watery splosh is heard as he hits the water. Me and Tez are up on feet in a flash looking into the drink but can't see anything.

"Where's he gone?" panics Tez, "Where's he gone?" and suddenly Foxy rises up coughing, spluttering and sort of shouting and screaming. "I can't!" and suddenly he's gone under again and then up again, "I can't, I can't," he's still shouting and sputtering and he's gone again and then he's back up again bobbing up and down like a fishing float on a rough sea and still shouting out the same old two words before he goes under again.

"Wonder what he's trying to say," I mused out aloud, "he can't what?"

"Foxy!" we shout at him, "Don't panic, don't panic. You could drown if you panic!"

And he's up again, "I am fuckin' drowning daft bastard,"

"There's no need to swear Foxy," says Tez.

"I can't!!" and he's gone again.

"Wish he'd stop bobbing up and down," I said, "I can't hear a word he's saying."

"You can't what Foxy?" Terry shouts at him.

And he's up again, "SWIM!!!I can't swim."

Terry looks at me, "He can't swim!"

"Just do doggy paddle Foxy!" I shout back and I'm looking at the water, "Oh he's gone again."

"You better go in and get him Ian," Terry announces to me like the decision is made.

"ME!" I snapped back, "Why me, you got the 100 meters and ya life saving badge."

"But you're a better swimmer than me, and you swam for school." Tez argues back.

"But that's at Madeley Street baths, not the Humber!" I said aloud. And Tez looks down at a man in certain distress, "If ya gonna go Ian, ya better do it now, because I bleedin aren't," was Tez's final word on the matter.

"Fuck!" I say and hurriedly rustle off my shoes and socks and am just about to dive in when Tez, says. "And it's full of shit down there, so I'd jump if were you. You don't want to go head first into a pile of turds and get a gob full." And, now thinking about Terry's words and suddenly I am not so keen, "Don't worry Foxy," I shout down at the black water, "I'll get a life belt."

Now you might believe reading this, that time is of the greatest urgency and we are arguing whilst poor old Foxy is drowning. But it didn't happen like that. All this palaver took place in the space of a few seconds and it just seems like a long time because you are reading it, but yes you are indeed right, Foxy is still drowning whilst we argue the toss. Then suddenly we become aware that all the splashing about has gone silent and old man Foxy is not be seen anywhere.

"Oh shit, he's gone under!" says Tez with a serious face.

"Oh God he's dead!" I announced out aloud. "I better ring 999 so they can recover the body if he's dead."

Then suddenly a voice comes out the Humber blackness below.

"No I'm not dead, you two useless bastards, but it's no thanks to

you two." And we both look down and Foxy is holding onto the remains of rotten ladder rung and we can just make him out. "Hang on there Foxy I'm gonna get a lifebelt!" and we both rush off in search of one of those red lifebelt boxes that use to be dotted all over the docks in those days. Now these life belt rings were made of like real heavy cork and they were monsters to carry for little kids like us but me and Tez managed to struggle one to the quayside. They also had a long rope tied to them. "Are you ready Foxy!"? we shouted and we threw it over and as luck would have it, Foxy had been quite right to have a bad feeling about this caper as he had mooched earlier. And it seemed as if the fates that night had it in for poor old Foxy because the life belt landed right smack on Foxy's noggin and he let out an almighty big yelp.
"ARE YOU TWO TRYING TO FINISH ME OFF YOU PAIR OF TWATS!!" he shouted along with all manner of other horrible words of abuse too disgusting for the delicate ears of Hull readers.

Now that's gratitude for you for saving his life, I thought. Me and Tez had all these visions of being on the front page of the Hull Daily Mail as the Lord Mayor presented us with bravery medals for valour and maybe even an audience with the Queen for saving old man Foxy from a watery grave at the bottom of Davy Jones locker. But it seemed alas it would be unlikely Foxy would put us forward for such a distinction given his somewhat ungrateful attitude. You just can't please some people can you?
But we did manage eventually to get the lifebelt around Foxy and started to pull Foxy out the water and heaved with all our might on the lifebelt rope and slowly but slowly Foxy began rise from the dark forbidden waters like an old sunken ghost ship. But you know when you think it just can't get any worse, and we have just pulled Foxy up to just below the big shit pipe and me and Tez are struggling to hold Foxy up, and Foxy is slipping back into the water, Foxy grabs hold of the opening on the shit pipe and is dangling off it, when would you believe it and bad luck strikes again. We were right after all, bad luck does come in threes. Suddenly the shit pipe starts up again and spews into action as

Foxy is dangling from the pipe and holding on like grim death and great mass of retching, stinky, slimy Hull turds by the ton pour over him like a sludgy brown tinted water fall. And he is not a happy man by any means, as it has been a bit of a bad day for Foxy to say the least. And you are left wondering those eternal questions of the universe that have mystified man through the ages, like. Just how can one man have so much bad luck in one night and seemingly have this strange attraction for two accidental encounters with shit, a lot of shit? But it wasn't all bad news, well when I say it wasn't all bad news, it was for Foxy, bit not for me and Tez. We did eventually, slowly but surely, manage to hoy him out the smelly Humber drink and when we did get him out he just stood there dripping wet and pebble dashed from head to foot in all manner shapes and sizes of big stinking Hull turds, coughing and spluttering his guts up, and he just sounded like one of those old Morris minor cars starting up on full choke on a cold and frosty morning. But would you believe it, the God's had taken mercy on Foxy at the last minute and he was still wearing his spiv trilby and it still had the little red feather sticking out the side. Sometimes you have to be grateful for small mercies, but we thought it better not to mention the small consolation as Foxy had taken on somewhat of silent mood and seemingly sent us to Coventry and when we inquired as to his well being, he just looked at me and Tez with this face, and on it was an expression often described as a glare of daggers. "It was just an accident Foxy," said Tez.

"I did say Foxy, bad luck comes in threes." I put in my three pennies worth gently. "Are you alright Foxy?"

"Just, just," started Foxy slowly, "just, don't say another word. Please, just don't say another word."

And with Foxy in a mood, we all toddled off the docks in mutual silence with Foxy squelching and dripping with every step as he walked ahead of us grumbling and complaining to himself in front, some distance in front in fact, walking with the delicate gait of a cowboy who didn't know his horse had gone.

Chapter Eleven

THE BIG BOIL UP!

As the witch's poem goes.

Double, double toil and trouble;
Fire burn and caldron bubble.
Fillet of a fenny snake,
In the caldron boil and bake;
Eye of newt and toe of frog,
Wool of bat and tongue of dog,
Adder's fork and blind-worm's sting,
Lizard's leg and howlet's wing,
For a charm of powerful trouble,
Like a hell-broth boil and bubble.

Double, double toil and trouble;

The rickety old gas cooker is rattling away on full speed ahead and all gas rings have big old giant boiling pans on them bubbling away with steam pouring off them. And so many shrimps have we caught, that Foxy has dragged an old copper boiler from the bag yard, and plugged it in without it managing for it to go bang or put the street lights out, and it too is now full of shrimps with steam pouring off and also shaking and rather ominously I thought, rattling away as it on full power and gibbering like an old boiler ready to blow up. So much steam is there, that it is as thick as Humber fog on frosty night in Foxy's back kitchen. And for the first time in our lives Foxy doesn't have his overcoat on, but with his jumper sleeves rolled up and his wife's kitchen pinny on, Foxy is stood up on an old chair, with one foot on the gas cooker, stirring the mix with an old cricket bat and laughing to him self like an evil old witch round a caldron preparing a spell.
"Eh Foxy," Tez shouts over, "You look like Fanny Craddock!"

"You two never stop taking the piss do you!" says Foxy unamused, "You two could learn somfink here," says Foxy all engrossed, "You are watching a master at work now," says Foxy as he stirs some more.

Me and Terry too are taking it in turns too to stir the old copper boiler with a baseball bat and we've bought about ten packets of Saxa sea salt to stir in for taste.

Now I don't know if you readers know this but something very odd happens when you add salt to pans full of shrimps on the boil and we didn't know it either. So being rookies in the shrimp boiling game and we pour in the salt and the next we knew, these shrimps are jumping out the pans and popping all over the place like ricocheting bullets and bouncing and jumping all over the kitchen floor and me and Tez are dodging about trying to avoid the flying shrimps. And talk about stink, now I don't know about Tez and I don't know about Foxy, but the smell coming off those boiling pans didn't give me a lot of confidence these shrimps were exactly safe to eat. And I could see Terry and Foxy beginning to back away from the steamy stink.

"Bloody 'ell," Tez cringed as he back away wafting with his hands. "Now that's a stink Foxy."

"What you on about?" says Foxy, "I can't smell anything." And Foxy gets out this big dirty great wooden stew spoon and like a master chef testing the soup, scoops out a load of steaming shrimps and looks at them. They are still a mucky grey colour.

"I thought they'd go pink by now," says Tez all curious. And then Foxy shoves the shrimp full wooden spoon into his mouth and starts munching and crunching away, and me and Tez cringe with yukky faces. "You supposed to pull off the head and tail first Foxy, aren't you?"

And Foxy then swallows. "Taste alright to me lads," and dunks the spoon back in the boil and shoves the spoon under mine and Tez's nose to sample. The colour just doesn't right and, the smell was enough to puke your guts up. I look at Tez and Tez looks at me.

"Well go on then!" Foxy shouts at us and we both tentatively pick one shrimp each off the spoon and tear the head, tail and legs off and carefully put it in our mouths and chew. And the more we chew, and, actually they don't taste that bad.

"Not bad," says Tez and he takes another one and I do too. "Mmmmm," I say like a Cordon bleu cook, "A dash more salt I think Foxy," and Foxy shovels in the salt all round the pans and the copper starts rattling and rolling and bubbling away some more. Another hour passes and we sample again. The taste is getting more and more like those shrimps you buy at the local wet fish shop, but the colour is just not that healthy luscious sea pink colour. They are still a shitty grey.

"They taste alright but we can't sell 'em that colour Foxy." I said. So we boiled them up some more, and then some more, and then some more, but as we poured in more salt, the taste got better but we just couldn't make the colour change. A few hours later and we are all sat around dumfounded and thinking hard. "We must be doing something wrong," says Foxy scratching his head.

"Just a minute says Tez," all of a sudden, "Have you got any pickled beetroot?"

"What for says?" says Foxy.

"Put in the boil," says Tez, "it'll dye 'em."

"Now that's a good idea," says Foxy and riffles his kitchen cupboards and out comes some dusty jars of pickled beet root and pickled red cabbage. Foxy blows off the dust, unscrews the lids and shoves the lot in and we all stir and stir and stir some more. And the colour of the shrimps starts to change but still not enough and there's no red cabbage or beetroot left. "Just a bit more and we're there," says Tez.

"What do we do now?" says Foxy sounding defeated. We all think some more. And then I had this brilliant idea. It was a eureka moment. "I know," I said suddenly standing up. "Me Mam once boiled our kids white T shirt with something red and it came out pink!"

"That's it!" said Foxy, "we'll dye the little bastards." And off Foxy rushed up stairs and after some rumbling came down with this big stinky red jumper and stirred it into one of the boiling pans as a test batch and we all stood there looking into the big pan and to our amazement after half an hour and the shrimps were slowly but surely changing colour and after an hour had turned a healthy sea side pink colour. "You're a genius Ian," said Tezza jumping about and we are all suddenly singing in chorus, "Money, money, money, money money."

For next few hours we are toiling away like Snow White's seven little dwarfs, "I HO, I HO IT'S OFF TO WORK WE GO." And we are using all the old red clothes we can find, shirts, jumpers, under pants, and stirring them into the boiling pans and copper boiler. All the shrimps are turning a really nice looking sea pink and for the last pan we have ran out of red clothes and Foxy takes off his shoes and red socks and stirs them into the last pan and me and Tez just look at each at in horror, "Just give that pan a wide berth," says Tez
"I suppose it'll be alright," I said trying to reassure myself more than anyone. "We are boiling them."
And so the night plods on and we are boiling, sieving and drying and by the time we finish and we are all knackered and me and Tez start to pour away all the water we have boiled the shrimps in.
"What ya doing?" Foxy snaps at us, "Our lass can use that as a stock for a nice shrimp curry." Me and Tez by this time are too tired to argue, we shrug our shoulders and leave Foxy to it.

Me and Tez crawl out of Foxy's house at three o'clock in the morning absolutely stinking of fish and Foxy's smelly house. Not the best of combination ordours. We have been bent over working so long our backs are aching and we can hardly straighten up, and we walk out of Foxy's gaff like two night blackened hunchbacks with our backs killing us. Terry slides off down the street on a north westerly course home and I go south. I sneak over the back wall as if me Mam catches me sneaking in at that time of night and I'll get a right pasting. I climb in through the back window and creep upstairs and into bed were my two brothers Colin and Graham are knocking out Z's and dead to the world, or so I thought, and I am no sooner snuggled up in my pit, and my brother Colin wakes and shouts, "Bloody 'ell what's that stink!" My brother Graham is still asleep. Remember now I'm the baby of the family and if my two big brothers pick on me, my Mam and big sister gives them a clout and especially my big brother bears that in mind before popping me one and so if anybody gets the blame, it's my quiet brother Graham, who never says boo to ghost and is a big goody, goody. So I pop my head out the covers and say, "It's bloody Graham, he's just let a big smelly one rip!" And my brother Colin throws a shoe at Graham that donks him with a big thud on the head and he wakes up, "What was that?" "You dirty smelly bastard!" My big brother Colin shouts at him, "You need to take a shit! It smells like something has crawled up you and died!"

And I pull the covers over my head with a snigger and minutes later after a hard night's toil, I am knocking out Z's too and I slip into dream land and I am driving a big car, and with a big beautiful bird sat in the passenger seat next to me, that oddly looks like Polo and Foxy is in the back wearing one of those millionair's fur coats and puffing on a big cigar adding up facts and figures. And Terry is in my dream too sat in the passenger seat counting big wads of juicy pound notes. In the dream I'm driving to our brand new shrimp factory and my two big brothers are working there as labourers, and Colin my eldest brother who never gives me any pocket money is sweeping the factory floor. And just as I'm getting to grips in my dream with this grown up bird that looks suspiciously like a good looking Polo, and things are hotting up and happening, and suddenly, the covers are pulled off me and Mam is shouting at me, "Get up you and get to school, and don't think of twagging because the boardman has got his eye on you my lad." And Mam pulls the covers right off and the cold morning air hits my warm little body, and dun't it always happen like that in dreams, as you're just getting down to business with a bird.

And me Mam pipes up with her face cringing, "What is that bleedin' stink?"

But I'm not feeling too well as my guts are bubbling a bit, "Aw Mam I don't feel too well," I groan.

"Don't try that one on me lad," Mam snaps back, "or you'll get a thick ear. Now get your arse up!"

And for the first time in my life of lies to get out of going to school, I was telling the truth, and as evidence of this I spent at least twenty minutes on the pot on the outside bog spluttering and trumping splashy ones over the bog pan with no end to the spluttering coming out my arse in sight.

But not even the pull of the outside bog and the rumble in my guts could keep me imprisoned morning. I had things to do, deals to make and people to see. I had it all planned, me and Tez would go to school get our attendance mark and as soon as we changed class we would do a "Snagger Puss", and as Snagger Puss the cartoon character would say, "Heavens to Murgatroyd!" and "Exit stage left even" and me and Tez would be out the door en route to the Fox residence. But something was certainly not right that morning and when Tez turned up at my house that morning for school, he looked like a ghost, and so very oddly, he too had been sat on the pot emptying the contents of his guts down the pan.

But both of us were determined not to let anything stop us that morning. After all we were about to become millionaires, or so we thought. Talk about counting your chickens. Remember we were only little kids and little kids tend to get carried away.

We couldn't resist a knock on Foxy's door on our way to school but oddly no one answered and so we went back way and into his back yard and knocked on his back door, and voice cried out from the bog in the back yard and then followed by a rip roaring, machine gun-like splattering of sloppy farts coming from behind the door and I knocked on the bog door, "Are you in there Foxy?"

"In here!!" Foxy shouts back, "I've bin in here since four o' clock this morning. I've got an arse hole like a blood orange I can tell you."

Me and Tez look at each other, "Must be something catching," says Tez, "me and Ian have been on the bog all morning dropping splashy ones."

"Must be something we all ate," says Foxy's voice all curious through the bog door.

"Yeah," I said, "that's funny in it? But I can't think what?"

"Me neither," answers Foxy voice as he rips off a few more long noisy splashy raspers. "Anyway you two, fancy a bit of breakfast. I'm doing a bit of egg, bacon and shrimp."

"Eh Foxy," shouts Tez all indignant, "Don't you be eating all the profits."

"There's plenty more where they come from," Foxy shouts back, "Our lass is doing a shrimp curry for tea if you two fancy a bit later."

"Never bleedin' mind shrimp curry," Tez shouts back through the door, "just get of your arse of the bog and start flogging 'em, and we'll be back later."

Neither me or Tez are feeling too good that morning and I can hear Tez's guts rumbling and mine are too and suddenly me and Tez are looking at each other eyes wide open because something is starting to squeeze out from between our buttocks. And you know when you have that frightening feeling of powerlessness and that no matter how hard you try to squeeze your arse together this is only going to end in a messy disaster and you know with certainty you are about to shit yourself, well that was exactly the feeling. And we both grab two old buckets in Foxy's back yard and whip down our kegs and next you know we both sat on the buckets rasping and bubbling away for next ten minutes. And what with all three of us noisily rasping and grinding away, it must have sounded like an out of tune church organ with broken pipes being played in Foxy's back yard.

Now me and Tez know what you readers are now thinking, 'What will we use for toilet paper?' But we are Hessle Road kids and always rough and ready and any of the old rags lying about in Foxy's yard is as good as any bog roll for the likes of us and having cleaned our eyes out, we pull up pants having done the dastardly deed and having blasted out what little now was left in our guts, we did feel a bit better. Our kegs now back up, and still the penny isn't dropping, and we shout back through Foxy's bog door, "We'll be back later Foxy!"

"Alright Lads," Foxy shouts back followed by more loud rasping farts from behind the bog door. "As soon as I'm off the pot, I'll start selling them door to door round the street. They'll go like hot shit off a stick."

And me and Tez, still both feeling a tad bubbly in the guts department toddle off to school with plans to be back very soon to help sell our ill-gotten shrimp booty and share out the cash.

Everything went according to plan when we got to school and we were out the gates not long after going in the gates. But the best laid plan of mice and men sometimes do not work out, and me and Tez are pelting down Boulevard with a spring in our step and our little legs going ten to the dozen, when the ominous sound of, pop, pop, pop is coming up on the inside behind us, and we look back and hot on our trail is old Ted Key, the school board man and he's getting closer. So we bolt down a nearby alley, over a back garden wall, bomb down a ten foot, short cut across some gardens and down some more back alleys, shimmy up a drain pipe and climb up on a house roof, run across and jump from roof to roof, slide down another drain pipe and just like the Milk Tray Man, "All because they lady loves Milk Tray" and we are two streets away now and puffing and panting like fagged out old nag race horses and we sneak round corner laughing to each other for cleverly giving old Ted Key the slip like two sneaky convicts on the run.

And we had just finished congratulating ourselves when who do we walk straight into sat on his moped casually puffing on his pipe but the "Marshal Matt Dillon" of Boulevard High School the school board man Ted Key, "You two took your time lads," he says with a clever smile, and the smile soon goes and, "Stand up straight!" he barks at us, "You two horrible little men, ABOUT TURN! Now at the double MARCH! Get them knees up lad, get them knees up!" In those days everybody was ex Army and acted like sergeant majors with us kids. And he paces us on his moped bawling and shouting like the evil Sergeant Snudge out of the TV series Bootsy and Snudge, and marches me and Tez straight into the head master's office and it's bend over and the whistling swish of cane goes through the air and it's, WHACK! WHACK! WHACK! And with our arses stinging with six of best, we are frog marched back to class by the scruff of our necks and plonked down unceremoniously at a desk. "And if either of you two disappear during the day, I'll know about it, and I'll hunt you down. UNDERSTAND!!"

"Yes, sir!" Me and Tez says in a chorus.

And Ted Key leans into our faces, take out his pipe from the corner of his mouth and blows his smoke right in my face, "Yes, Sir, that's right Sir," he snaps at us with a vengeance, "You horrible little creatures! I'm watching you Achmed and I've got my beady eye on you too Cox!"

Chapter Twelve

So it's play time at school, and as daft as it sounds, even though we were now in first year senior school we still called it play time. I am sat in trap one in the school bogs and Terry is sat in trap two and in-between burst of machine gun fire coming out of our arses, we are talking business. "There can't be that much left up there now," I say with a heavy groan, and no sooner had the words left my lips and another burst echoes round the school bogs.
"I must have lost a couple of stone," groans Terry.
I am groaning too, "It must have been something we ate."
"I bet it was those chips we bought from the chip shop the other night," says Tez dropping another sploshy load.
"I'm never buying owt from that fish shop again!" I moaned and it was bombs away again. And even through all this bad guts agony, I start sniggering to myself with other thoughts, "But think of all that lovely money Tez."

The last lesson was maths with a teacher called Foo Foo because he looked like the TV cartoon character. He was a bit of animal and if you played him up sticks of chalk and even boards rubbers would often go flying across the classroom and often kids got their heads split open as it cracked your head. But you never complained because you'd get a good belting off your parents for messing about at school if you did.

Me and Tez were eagerly watching the clock for 4 o'clock and it seemed the closer it got to 4 o'clock the slower the dials seemed to move. We had business to do and now school was in the way. Then suddenly the sound of another classroom door opens and closes with a slam and the school bell monitor is running down the corridors and Foo Foo dismisses us, and I get a massive clout on the noggin as I pass him. "And remember Accccccchhhhhmed, six of the best if you're late in morning."
Foo Foo always mocked my surname with a growling throaty, "Acccccchhhhhhmed." But I didn't mind because he took the piss out everybody. It wasn't a racial thing.

But me and Tez never got to the school gates but bolted straight for the school bogs again and emerged half an hour later looking absolutely thin and drawn having had another episode of emptying our our guts. And when we got to Foxy's house and he hadn't even started flogging the shrimps. He's on the pot again blasting out more big splashy ones from behind his back yard karsi door. "Eh Foxy," I shout through the door, "What you doing in there?"

"Oh lads," Foxy groans back, "I don't feel too well lads."

"Never mind excuses Foxy!" Tez shouts back. "Let's get selling." And suddenly after a rattle of the bog chain and a watery flush Foxy emerges. "I feel better after that," says Foxy with a huff of great relief. "There can't be much more left up there, I can tell ya." And we all mosey on inside and Foxy's ugly fat Missis is slaving over a hot stove with a big dirty pan on the gas stove stirring.

"Fancy a drop of shrimp stew lads?" says Foxy. And me and Tez had to admit, it didn't smell too bad and so Foxy dished it up and we all got stuck in dipping our bread in.

"Promise Lads," says Foxy getting slopping up his shrimp stew, "I'll make a start first thing in the morning. My guts are playing me up something rotten. I've been on and off the pot all day."

"Now that's funny," says Tez, "So have me and Ian. I bet it's something we ate."

"Must be something going round," says Foxy. "Even my lad's got it, and our lass has been shitting through the eye of a needle as well."

"It must something they ate like us then," says Tez quick off the mark.

"Well I can't fink what," says Foxy. "All my lad had to eat was a shrimp sandwich and me and our lass had a drop of shrimp curry for dinner. Lovely with a bit of boiled rice."

"Strange that innit?" I said gobbling up my shrimp stew. "I wonder what it is?" and we all looked at each other.

"This shrimp stew is hitting the spot," says Tez chucking it down his neck. "Any way at least we can get selling the shrimps around the street tomorrow." And Tez laughs all evil and greedy like, "All that lovely lolly is something to look forward to."

That night neither me Terry, Foxy, his lad or his lass got any sleep it would transpire, and all of us virtually camped out in the back yard bog and by this time all our arse holes were like squashed grapes. But like the soldiers we were, me and Tez were up early and off to school just dropping in at Foxy's for a few minutes for a moral boosting team talk. And yet again the conversation would be through Foxy's bog door.

"Right Foxy!" Tez demanded through the door, "you make a start and we'll be back to help after school." And after a massive long rattle of more heavy and prolonged sploshy 'Machine gun' fire from behind the bog door me and Tez looked at each other and cringed, "See ya later Foxy," and we were off to school. And for once we were early and who should be waiting for us in the class room but the school board man Ted Key, in his Mackintosh, Trilby and his Sherlock Holmes's pipe hanging from the corner of his mouth and puffing on it like a steam train, "Well done lads," he barked at us, "Credit where credits due," but still took no prisoners, "I'll be right here in the morning and every morning." And Ted stared us down, "You two step out of line and I'll drop on you like a ton of bricks."

"Yes sir!" me and Tez jumped to it.

"Yes, sir!" Ted Key snapped back and was gone like an evil genie.

It was another 'on the bog ground hog day' for me and Tez and we were in and out of the classroom all day running back and forwards emptying our guts and back again like bleedin' yoyos. Eventually I had made a school record and had two full days in at school for one week and then at 4 o clock it was the long awaited home time.

When we got to Foxy's for a change he wasn't on the bog but sat in his back kitchen with a big self satisfied smirk on his face and there were no shrimps to be seen anyway.

"I flogged the lot door to door!" announced Foxy. "Went like hot cakes."

Me and Tez's eyes popped out our head, "How much did we make?" me and Tez asked together in a greedy little chorus.

And Foxy's tone suddenly changed to much harsher tone "That's something we'll have to talk about lads?' And it had all the sounds of a rip-off coming, and it was. He peeled off two five pound notes from a big roll in his pocket and handed one to me and one to Terry. "That's your share lads."

"But we agreed," I piped up like a daft lad. "A three way split."

"After what you two piss takers put me through the other night," said Foxy leering at us, "Ya' both lucky to get that."

"Well," said Tez snapping back all threatening, "We'll see what our our kid has to say about this."

"And my big brother as well. He will punch ya lights out Foxy!" I also piled in with another threat.

Foxy has this sneaky smile on his face and just grins back, "Oh yeah," says Foxy looking at me, "And suppose Polo's Dad finds out what you and Polo have been up to. Ya dirty little sod."

"I haven't been up to anything with Polo," I said going all red and lying very badly.

"That's not what I hear," Foxy reparts cleverly, "And what will ya Mam says eh?"

"Well," says Tez, "That's him and not me. Our kid will still kick ya head in Foxy."

"Oh yeah," Foxy turns on Tez, "And what will ya Mam and Dad say Coxy," says Foxy cleverly to Tez, "When she finds out about the eel ya threw into Sweaty Betty's bedroom. Never mind what Sweaty Betty will do when finds out and gets her hand on you both."

And suddenly me and Tez have been stopped in our tracks and we gulp and we suddenly have no more threats to make.

"And," Foxy added, "I'm taking over the shrimp business and the partnership is dissolved," he said with a little evil laugh. "Now I'll keep your secrets and you just keep out'a the shrimping game."

Foxy had check mated us and there wasn't a damn thing we could do about it and me and Tez slunk out of Foxy's house and we could hear him laughing as we left.

"It's all your fault!" Tez snapped at me, "Messing about with Polo."

"And what about you?" I shouted back, "And the eel in Sweaty Betty's bed, that was your idea!"

"Well you could have stopped me," said Tez.

"Me!" And we walked down the street arguing and blaming each other for being ripped off by Foxy.

That night I lay in bed thinking about all the lovely money me and Tez had been ripped off by and plotted every manner of horrible stuff I was going to do on Foxy. And just like Tez had said it would, my antics with Polo had come to haunt me and now Foxy would have me over a barrel for eternity, and Tez too. But as far as Polo was concerned I was definitely cured. The hot snogging and pressing sessions were definite over...I think. But at least there was one good thing me and Tez were spending less and less time on the bog. But funnily enough Foxy was still suffering from an acute case of the shits, or so street rumour had it. But why should we care. It was curious though but I never thought about it for long.

Whilst me and Tez had fell out blaming each other for getting ripped off, we were still mates and Terry called for me early the next morning for school.

It was strangely quiet that morning and the deathly silence in the street struck us both. Something very odd and curious was going on that morning I have to say. Yes, something very odd indeed. The whole street was empty and deathly quiet and there was this stink, not unlike a Mumbai sewer on a hot day. And even weirder, there was absolutely nobody around, no one on their bikes going to work, no kids going to school. The whole street was like the Mary Celeste. "That's funny," and I asked Tez as we walked to school, "Where is everybody?" And as we walked down the street you could hear a pin drop, and then there was this odd metallic sound of like mass toilet chains being pulled and bogs being flushed. We never gave it another thought and off we toddled to school. Then when we got to school, it was even stranger, none of the kids from our street were at school either. Now that was odd, really odd. But being little kids, you don't tend to think much on such things and so we merrily plodded along through the day and through, maths class and through boring history and geography, and thankfully sighing and looking at the clock, it came to 4pm and the bell goes and we bolt for home. But the closer we get to our street and we can hear people shouting, angry people and as we get closer to our street, crowds are out and strangely all around the Foxy's Terrace. Some little kid is running down the street and we stop him, "What's going on?"

"There's gonna be a riot. Foxy has given everybody the shits," says this little kid, "and there gonna kill him. But he won't come out'a his house."

Me and Tez just suddenly looked at each other like in revelation and said in chorus, "IT WAS THE SHRIMPS!"

We ran down the street like the wind, and could not help the thought, was this justice or what, and, hadn't we got off lightly. When we got to Foxy's terrace a mob had gathered outside and were banging on his door, and the language, and the threats. The air was blue with every manner of profanity known to man.

Sweaty Betty was shouting her gob off, "I knew something was wrong this morning when my Bert shit the bed. He hasn't done that for months!"

"My Harry, has been on the pot since six this morning," shouted Nimphy Nora. "That bog seat has probably scared him for life." And she shouted through Foxy's letter box, "Come out Foxy!, ya bastard!, We want a word with you!"

"My Ted's the same," says this other woman fuming with anger. "My Teds lost a day's pay and he daren't fart 'cause he keeps following through. He's artexed the inside of underpants three times today and is still on the pot blasting away and his arse is like a grapefruit."

Now all though we would like to try and give as good a description of events as we can, the language would be unrepeatable for the ears of our delicate readers and we will relay here just a small sample of the verbal abuse, threats and all manner of bad behaviour aimed at Foxy's house. "I'm gonna kill him!" "Come out you bastard!" "You just wait till I get my hands on you!" And words and phrases of that ilk were generally being banded about with abundance and gay abandon. But still there was no sign of the man of the moment, Signor Foxy.

Yes, Foxy was definitely keeping his head down, or so it seemed, that was for sure and who could blame him because gatherings like this are often described in the cowboy movies as an unruly lynch mob and I think that description would be very fitting in this case. And under the circumstance, if Foxy was keeping his head down inside, I think that would be the right decision until the heat was off anyway. But credit where credit's due and this unruly mob were certainly determined to get their pound of flesh I will give them that. And I don't think even Foxy could ignore what came next as a group of very big blokes came down the terrace carrying a battering ram for his front door, and if you have ever seen that film, "The Vikings" well that's what it was like, but I don't think they had rape and pillage on their mind, just a large measure of GBH and common assault I think was on their minds. And with a big cheer came the first big crash of the battering ram on Foxy's front door. And suddenly Foxy knows the game is up and he comes to his bedroom window to address the masses and he is as usual wearing his iconic trilby. And big violent jeer goes up from the crowd just like when the robber Bill Sykes took the roof in the film Oliver Twist.

"Come down here Foxy!" shouts this bloke steaming mad. "I want a word with you."

"Well put the base ball bat down then," Foxy shouts back.

Now I know we shouldn't get smug, but me and Tez did get a feeling of self satisfaction seeing Foxy get his comeuppance for ripping off us two little innocent kids just trying to make ends meet. And we couldn't resist the odd shout up at Foxy to take the piss at his difficult position.

"Eh Foxy," Tez shouts up, "Get ya'self one of them pointy hats and you'll look like the Pope."

Then Foxy turns to us stood in the crowds below, "Eh it wasn't just me," he points at us, "them two were in on it as well."

Me and Tez are so shocked now, Foxy has sunk to a new low and is blaming poor little kids. Not that trying to blame us did Foxy any good. As far as the mob was concerned it had been Foxy who had flogged them the shrimps and his name was quite clearly on the tin as it were.

Someone did eventually call the Police, and an ambulance as well because Foxy did eventually come down from the pulpit and as daft as it sounds was caught making a bolt for it out his back way. But alas he did not get far and Hessle Road justice was served up in full measure and the ambulance it seems had been well anticipated by some thoughtful soul and on stretcher Foxy was carted to Hull Royal with blue lights flashing. Later the crowds' dissipated and an edgy bog smelly calm descended on the street.

Yes, for quite a few days our street smelled like a blocked sewer what with all the residents dropping their guts either in the outside bog, or stopping in the street to very, very gingerly fart just in case there was anything more sinister lurking behind and they shit themselves. Because let's face diarrhea can be one sneaky little devil and what can seem in all innocence like just small fart rumbling its way to the exit and the next thing you know you have filled your under kegs with a big sloppy smelly wet one that starts sliding down your leg.

Now although we are nearing the end of this sad tale, it is not quiet over yet and just out of interest me and Tez had cause to go back to Foxy's house later that night and inside his antiques emporium had been well and truly trashed. But there standing in the corner like a little lost lonesome soul in the dark mayhem, was Foxy's Russian bear. And suddenly we remembered where Foxy hid his stash; up the bear's jacksey and whilst trying to show at least some respect for the bear, Tez stuck his hand up and indeed Foxy's stash somewhat smelly was pulled out. We didn't take the lot, but split it three ways just as in our gentlemen's agreement and it came to a handsome sum 25 quid each. But me and Tez hadn't quit finished with the bear yet and we both looked at each other sniggering.

And later that night as The Milky Bar Kid was strolling home pissed from Criterion Pub he got the shock of his life when me and

Tez pushed the bear out of a dark alley and growled at him and he had never run so fast in his life. And so, the next morning and The Milky Bar Kid is telling every body about his scary encounter, "I tell you it was a fuckin' bear. Massive it was with these big teeth, and big scary claws," and every body just rolled their eyes, "And I suppose it was with a pink elephant was it! Silly bastard!," said Work Shy Cyril. And another legend was born down the street, that of the Ghost of the "Midnight Bear" that stalked the lonely streets of Marmaduke Street in the twilight hours.

Now I'm afraid it's the end of this tale down the street of misfits, for now anyway. Suffice to say, that although me and Tez were best friends, we did have a bit of a big fall out and I'm only telling this story so you will know what a little sneak Terry Cox is.
You might remember that Terry always professed to have my best interests at heart when it came to my cavorting sessions with Polo. And whilst I kept to my word for many weeks and resisted whatever temptations Polo threw at me through thick and thin, I was weakening by the day. One night my young loins were getting the better of me and pulling me, slowly but surely, closer and closer towards Polo's front door as I had heard her Mam and Dad were in the Criterion Pub. I really hated myself but just couldn't help it. Again I was backsliding on my oath to Tezza and in a frenzy of frustration I found myself in desperation knocking on Polo's door for release from the now bulging urges of nature. But to my horror there was no answer, and when I came to think about it, Polo had not bothered me for some weeks now, and Terry also was disappearing with an all too frequent regularity. Anyway, I peered through Polo's front room window and to my absolute horror and disappointment there was my best mate, Tez and Polo on the front room couch with Tez getting all the benefits usually reserved for me. THE BASTARD!!

The next day Tez as usual called for me for school and I never said a word about Polo and Tez was also quiet as well, and he was wearing a big fat lip and a black eye. I thought it imprudent at the time to enquire with Tez how said injuries had been acquired.

But apparently there had been something of a rucas at Polo's house the night before when some boy had been found in the throws of passionate indiscretion with Polo on her front room couch. Some spiteful person it transpired had gone to the pub and told Polo's dad what was going on his couch with his daughter Polo.

"Mmmmm, I wonder who it was?" Chuckle, chuckle, snigger, snigger.

And suffice to say thereafter, I would assume my rightful place back on Polo's couch with all the benefits that entailed and was no longer worried about going blind and Terry it seemed joined Radish and Whispering Jack back on the "hand pump" by candle light.

THE END?...FOR NOW THAT IS.